Language and the Teacher:
A Series in Applied Linguistics

Volume 2

under the editorial direction of

DR. ROBERT C. LUGTON

American Language Institute of New York University

LANGUAGE AND THE TEACHER:
A SERIES IN APPLIED LINGUISTICS

The series will be concerned with the following areas—

GENERAL STUDIES
Psycholinguistics, sociolinguistics, bilingualism.

GRAMMAR
Morphology, syntax, contrastive structure.

PHONOLOGY
Phonemics, intonation, contrastive phonetics, etc.

VOCABULARY STUDIES
Frequency counts, production and principles, lexicology.

READING SKILLS
Beginning skills, development, construction of texts, literary reading.

WRITING SKILLS
Beginning skills, development, composition.

METHODOLOGY
Evaluation of methods, techniques, classroom practices.

**LANGUAGE TEACHING
FOR DIFFERENT AGE GROUPS**
Elementary, secondary, college, adult.

MACHINE TEACHING
Programmed learning, audio-visual equipment and software, language laboratory.

TEACHER EDUCATION
Standards and evaluation, projects, curricula for teacher training

ADMINISTRATION
Curriculum development, articulation, public relations.

TESTING
Techniques, statistical studies.

BIOGRAPHY

BIBLIOGRAPHY

ENGLISH AS A SECOND LANGUAGE

**METHODS OF RESEARCH IN LINGUISTICS
AND LANGUAGE TEACHING**

Language and the Teacher:
A Series in Applied Linguistics

Practice-Centered Teacher Training

— Spanish —

by

Diana E. Bartley

Assistant Professor, Curriculum and Instruction
School of Education
The University of Wisconsin, Milwaukee

and

Robert L. Politzer

Professor of Education and Romance
Linguistics, and Research and Development Associate,
Stanford Center for Research and Development
in Teaching

THE CENTER FOR CURRICULUM DEVELOPMENT, INC.
401 Walnut Street   Philadelphia, Pa.

#2576

Originally issued as Technical Report #2
Stanford Center for Research and
Development in Teaching pursuant to a
contract with the Office of Education, H.E.W.

Table of Contents

Introduction

PRACTICE-CENTERED TEACHER TRAINING: SPANISH

A Syllabus for the Training or Retraining of Teachers of Spanish[*]

One of the most important developments in foreign language education during the last decade has been the retraining of foreign-language teachers in various types of institutes and the development of tests designed to measure the competence necessary for foreign-language teachers. These tests, commonly known as the MLA (ETS) Tests for Advanced Students and Teachers, measure competence in (1) language skills (speaking, reading, writing, oral comprehension), (2) applied linguistics, (3) teaching methodology (professional preparation), and (4) civilization and culture. They are based on the Modern Language Association recommendations as to qualifications of the secondary-school teacher of Modern Languages (PMLA vol. 70, No. 4, Part 2, pp. 46–49, September, 1955) and they correspond quite well to what are considered the essential elements of the specific preparation of the modern-language teacher. They define, in a sense, not only the curriculum used in the retraining of foreign-language

[*]The research and development reported in this syllabus was performed pursuant to a contract with the United States Department of Health, Education, and Welfare, Offiice of Education, under the provisions of the Cooperative Research Program.

teachers, but also the essential element of foreign-language teacher training generally speaking.

The retraining and, to some extent, the original training of the foreign-language teacher then takes the form of courses in language, culture and civilization, applied linguistics and methods. To these courses is added an element of practice: observation, student teaching, practice teaching, internship, etc. In many cases, especially in the original training of the teacher, the courses and the practical experience are related in various sequential patterns. Quite typically, the courses follow each other and are in turn followed by the practical experience.

In the case of retraining in institutes, courses and practice are usually parallel experiences. The amount of integration between the courses, and between courses and the practice element, varies a great deal depending on a variety of circumstances. The schema of a teacher-training or retraining institute may thus be represented as follows:

Lessons on:

Culture & Civilization	Language Practice	Applied Linguistics	Methods	Practical Experience

The aims of this teacher-training syllabus are (1) to bring about a much closer integration of the language practice, applied linguistics, and methods element of the teacher-training courses, and (2) relate them directly to the practice element by introducing the device of "micro-teaching."

Micro-teaching is a technique of teacher training which was developed in the Stanford University Secondary Teacher Training program. It consists in having the apprentice teacher teach small 5-to-10-minute lessons to a small group of students (5 to 10). The students are usually paid subjects, but chosen in such a way that they can actually participate in and profit from the lessons to be taught. The micro-lesson itself focuses on a specific teaching skill which is to be learned by the apprentice teacher.

This syllabus is based on the concept that in the teacher-training program, each lesson in applied linguistics (I) is linked to a corresponding lesson in language practice (if needed by the trainee), that these are related to principles of methodology (II), and that all of these experiences are applied in specific micro-lessons (III) to be taught by participants in the training program. The structure of the training procedure may thus be presented in the following way.

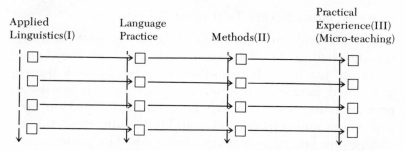

Applied Linguistics(I) Language Practice Methods(II) Practical Experience(III) (Micro-teaching)

In other words, the emphasis of the training procedure shifts from a "vertical" progression, patterned according to parallel or sequential courses, to a "horizontal" progression, in which elements of individual courses are integrated with each other and in which the practical teaching experience rather than the final examinations in each course presents the goal toward which the individual elements are pointed.

The syllabus consists, therefore, of the following three parts.

PART I: APPLIED LINGUISTICS

This section of the syllabus contains a very brief outline of some of the main facts of Spanish structure and the main points of interference coming from English. Part I of this syllabus is not meant to replace any of the existing manuals on applied linguistics. It is primarily a guide for the person responsible for teacher training—not a textbook for the trainee. It does not contain a complete description of Spanish structure, nor does it purport to present a complete contrastive analysis of Spanish and English. Part I is, however, followed by a brief index to applied linguistics manuals.

Language Practice

If the trainee is himself in need of a review of the essentials of Spanish grammar, it is of course advisable to present the review in such a fashion that it is integrated with the applied linguistics materials. Such a presentation will necessitate careful cooperation between the instructor of the applied linguistics course and the instructor responsible for the language practice of the trainee.

PART II: SUGGESTED TEACHING BEHAVIORS

The Methods Section of the syllabus consists of a systematic listing of observable behaviors of the "good language teacher." It describes very briefly how the experienced language teacher conducts such activities as pronunciation drills, imparts knowledge of structure, controls classroom activities, etc., and it explains the rationale behind the language teacher's behavior. The performance criteria are based on observations made by the individuals responsible for the training of foreign language teachers within the Stanford University Secondary Teacher Training Program. These performance criteria are an instrument for the training as well as for the evaluation of the foreign language teacher. At the same time, however, it is clear that not *all* teachers can or should necessarily follow all of the suggestions made in Section II of this volume, but that each teacher or trainee must eventually develop his own optimal teaching style.

The teaching behaviors suggested in this volume were developed in the Stanford Teacher Training Program. Most of the beginning teachers following the program utilized the audio-lingual method and taught first-year courses. As a result, the teaching behaviors discussed in this volume reflect, undoubtedly, a bias toward the audio-lingual method. The origin and background of the suggested teaching behaviors also account for the fact that certain problems of teaching methodology are not discussed because they do not represent the problem of the beginning language teacher (e.g., the sequencing of materials—which is, in fact, provided by the textbook—or the teaching of composition — which is a problem for the more advanced levels of instruction).

PART III: MICRO-LESSONS

The series of sample micro-lessons shows how applied linguistics, knowledge of the language and specific performance criteria are combined into practical application. The micro-lessons described in this syllabus can be utilized in a variety of ways (which themselves are subject to experimental research). The apprentice teacher can be asked to teach one of the micro-lessons or can be asked to teach a micro-lesson modelled after the one formed in the syllabus. The micro-lesson of the syllabus can be used as a model presented first by an experienced teacher, then the trainee can be required to teach the identical or a similar lesson himself. Both the model performance of the experienced teacher and the performance of the trainee can be video-taped and the student can, under the guidance of his methods teacher or supervisor, be asked to compare the two performances. Just as in the language course and in the language laboratory we can concentrate on creating specific language skills through a process of modelling, imitating, repeating, etc., we can, in the micro-teaching procedure, focus on specific teaching skills.

The present Report was written by Mrs. Diana E. Bartley in collaboration with Professor Robert L. Politzer. Both authors wish to express their gratitude to Miss Margery A. Tudor, who rendered invaluable services in copy-editing and typing the final manuscript.

Stanford University
March, 1967

DIANA E. BARTLEY
ROBERT L. POLITZER

Part I. Applied Linguistics

I. PHONOLOGY

GLOSSARY OF TERMS used in phonology section of the manual of Applied Linguistics.

Articulators: The organs of the mouth (lips, teeth, etc.) used in producing a sound.

Point of articulation: The region of the mouth in which sounds are produced by the articulators effecting partial or complete closure characteristic of consonants.

Manner of articulation: At a certain point of articulation, sounds will differ in the way they are produced due to changes in the shape and size of various resonance cavities, or passages for the air stream of the articulators. Thus, several sounds may have the same point of articulation, but the manner of articulation for each of these will differ because its features are not the same.

Consonants are classified according to point and manner of articulation.

Points of articulation:

Bilabial: A bilabial sound is produced by the partial or complete closure of the upper and lower lips. /b, p, m, w/

Labiodental: The upper teeth and lower lip are brought together to form /f/.

I

Interdental: The tip of the tongue rests between the upper and lower teeth. /Θ/, [đ].

Dental: The tip of the tongue touches the back of the upper teeth. /d, t/

Alveolar: The tip of the tongue touches the upper gums. [s, z], /l, n, r, rr/

Palatal: The surface of the tongue touches the hard palate. /č, ļ, ñ, y/

Velar: The back part of the tongue touches or is held near the soft palate. /g/, /k/

Manners of articulation:

Stop: A stop sound is produced by the complete closure of the air passage followed immediately by the opening of the closure, causing the explosion of air, i.e., causing the stop sound. /b, p, t, d, k, g/

Continuants: Continuants are all sounds which are produced without complete stoppage of the air stream. [ƀ, đ, g], /f, Θ, H/

Fricative: Fricative sounds are formed by continuous friction produced in the narrowed air passage. [ƀ, đ, g], /f, Θ, H/ S-like sounds are often referred to as sibilants or groove fricatives. [s, z]

Affricate: An affricate is a stop sound and a fricative produced at the same point of articulation. Example: In English, /č/ is produced as follows: one first makes a sound similar to /t/ (a stop) which is followed by another sound similar to /š/.

Lateral: A lateral sound is one in which air is permitted to escape on either or both sides of the tongue. /l, ļ/

Nasal: When the air passage in the nose is open rather than the air passage in the mouth, a nasal sound is produced. /m, n, ñ/, [η]

Trill: A trill is produced by a vibration of the tongue (or lips or uvula) caused by the passage of air. /rr/ as in /perro/

Flap: A flap is produced by a rapid movement of the tongue across the alveolar ridge, /r/ as in /pero/

Semiconsonant: A semiconsonant is a continuant sound which has the characteristics of both consonant and vowel.

Features:

Voiced: The presence of vibration of vocal chords during the production of a consonant produces a voiced sound. /b, g/

Unvoiced: The absence of vibration of vocal chords during the production of a consonant produces an unvoiced sound. /p, k/

Symbols:

Throughout the phonology and morphology sections, the following symbols are used:

/ / = phoneme
[ ] = allophone (variant)
{ } = morpheme
⟨ ⟩ = grapheme (written symbol)*

LIST OF REFERENCES USED FOR THE GLOSSARY

Francis, W. Nelson. *The Structure of American English*. New York, 1958.

Gleason, H. A. *An Introduction to Descriptive Linguistics*. New York, 1955.

Hill, Archibald A. *An Introduction to Linguistic Structures*. New York, 1958.

Navarro Tomás, Tomás. *Manual de Pronunciación Española*. 5th ed. Hafner, New York, 1957.

Pei, Mario A. and Frank Gaynor. *Dictionary of Linguistics*. New York, 1954.

Politzer, Robert L. and Charles N. Staubach. *Teaching Spanish, A Linguistic Orientation*. 2nd ed. New York, 1965.

A. CONSONANTS:

Bilabials: /p/ /b/ /m/ /w/

/p/ (unvoiced bilabial stop) In initial position in Spanish it is always unaspirated, whereas in English it is aspirated. It normally does *not* occur in final position.

---

* NOTE: The symbol ⟨ ⟩ will also be used to indicate orthography and also to set off words in the sentence in which they are being discussed.

/b/

[b]   (voiced bilabial stop) In initial position or following /m/ or /n/, it is comparable to its English counterpart.

[ƀ]   (voiced bilabial fricative) A [ƀ] occurs in any other position where [b] does not occur. It is made by keeping the lips slightly apart without impeding the flow of air.

/m/   (voiced bilabial nasal) It is comparable to its English counterpart in all positions. (see /n/ for /n/-to-/m/ substitutions)

/w/   (voiced bilabial semiconsonant) It is comparable to its English counterpart. (It is sometimes considered voiced velar semiconsonant, but because the lips can be considered the principal articulators, it will be included with bilabials.)

Labiodentals: /f/

/f/   (voiceless labiodental) It is comparable to its English counterpart as in father.

The orthographic symbol ⟨v⟩ corresponds to the voiced bilabial stop [b] and fricative [ƀ]. In Spanish, there is no voiced ladiodental sound as there is in English.

Dental and Interdental: /t/   /ϴ/   /d/

/t/   (voiceless dental stop) The Spanish /t/ differs from the English /t/ in that it is produced by placing the tongue against the back of the teeth, whereas in English, the tongue is placed against the alveolar ridge. In Spanish, it is always unaspirated, while in English it is aspirated. In Spanish, it normally does not occur in final position.

/ϴ/   (voiceless interdental fricative) It is used by Castilian speakers as the sound which corresponds to the symbols ⟨c⟩ and ⟨z⟩. The Spanish /Θ/ is more lenis than the English /Θ/. Otherwise, the manner of production is comparable.

[d] (voiced dental stop) It is produced by placing the tongue behind the teeth, whereas in English the tongue is placed on the alveolar ridge. [d] is produced initially after /m/, /n/ or /l/.

/d/

[đ] (voiced interdental fricative) It is a sound somewhat like the English [đ] of lather.

Alveolars:

[s] (unvoiced alveolar fricative; also referred to as groove fricative) It is comparable to the English/s/. Intervocalically, the Spanish ⟨s⟩ corresponds to [s] and not to /z/ as in English. (e.g., he ha*s* a hat) = (/hi haz ə hæt/)

/s/

[z] (voiced alveolar fricative; also referred to as groove fricative) It is comparable to the English /z/ as in zebra. The Spanish [z] does not correspond to the orthographic symbol ⟨z⟩ of Spanish but rather to the [s] of Spanish before a voiced consonant.

(e.g., los dueños venecianos) = (lo*z* dweño*z* benecyanos)

/l/ (voiced alveolar lateral) In producing the English /l/, the tongue assumes a hollow or concave shape, low at the base. There are several variants of the English /l/, none of which can be substituted for the Spanish /l/. One is produced against the alveolar ridge (as in "love") and the other pronounced with the tongue raised against the back of the mouth (as in "bell"). Also, in some words, the [l] is reduced to a simple flap of the tongue ("black"). In Spanish, the tongue is rounded upward toward the upper gums and palate; the tip of the tongue touches the upper teeth.

/n/ This sound is comparable to the English /n/. The Spanish /n/ before /t/ becomes dental (antes, entonces), as it does in English (Anthony), and velar before velar consonants (see [ŋ]). The orthographic ⟨n⟩ before bilabial consonants, as in ⟨con Pedro⟩, becomes /m/, thus, /kom pedro/.

/r/ (voiced alveolar flap) It is produced by a rapid movement of the tip of the tongue (flapping of the tongue) across the alveolar ridge, touching it slightly.

/rr/ (voiced alveolar trill) The tip of the tongue, held against the alveolar ridge, is vibrated by the passage of air between the tongue and alveolar surfaces to form the trill. (The symbols /r̄/, /rr/ represent the trilled ⟨r⟩ of Spanish.)

Palatals:

/č/ (unvoiced palatal affricate) The sound is comparable in both English and Spanish.
(English ⟨church⟩, Spanish ⟨chino⟩) = (/čarc/, /čino/)

/ļ/ (voiced palatal lateral) (orthographic symbol ⟨ll⟩ as in calle) Contrary to general credence, the Spanish /ļ/ is not comparable to the English (or Spanish) sound orthographically represented by ⟨li⟩. English: alias: Spanish: aliado. To produce the Spanish /ļ/, the back of the tongue touches the roof of the mouth while the air escapes from each side as the sound is produced. In English and Spanish, the ⟨li⟩ /ly/ is produced by the tip of the tongue touching the alveoli followed by the semiconsonant /y/.

(aliado /alyaďo/; millón /milyən/) In some areas of Spain and Latin America the /ļ/ has merged with /y/.

/ñ/   A similar phenomenon occurs with /ñ/. The /ñ/ is not to be confused with the /ny/ of the Spanish word ⟨uranio⟩. The difference is that to produce the /ñ/, the front of the tongue presses against the hard palate as the air escapes through the nasal cavity. Practically, at once, the tongue moves away from the hard palate producing a short fricative [y] sound. In /ny/, the tip of the tongue touches the upper gums followed by the semiconsonant /y/.

/y/   (voiced palatal semiconsonant) The pronunciation of the initial /y/ as in ⟨yo⟩ has three variations. The two most commonly heard are [j] (comparable to English Joe) and [y] (as in yes). The third, [ž] (as in treasure) is common to Argentines and Uruguayans. The native speakers of English must learn that in Spanish, these are variants of one phoneme. Intervocalically, there are two variants: [y], [ž].

Velars:

/k/   (unvoiced velar stop) This sound is comparable to its English counterpart.

/H/   (unvoiced velar fricative) This sound is somewhat different from the /h/ in American English. In Spanish, the tongue is higher in the mouth and tenser than in English, so that friction produced is against the velum.

[g]   (voiced velar stop) This sound is comparable to its English counterpart.

/g/

[g]   (voiced velar fricative) This sound does not have an English counterpart. The back of the

tongue does not touch the velum but rather gets close enough to permit the continuous passage of air without impeding it. The [g] occurs inter-vocalically (or follows vowels), follows all con-sonants except ⟨m⟩ and ⟨n⟩, and occurs in syllable final position. Orthographically, the [g] is equivalent to ⟨g + a, o, u⟩ or ⟨gu + i, e⟩ in any of the above mentioned positions.

/n/ → [ŋ] (voiced velar nasal)   In Spanish, the ⟨n⟩ before a velar consonant (finca, sangre) becomes a velar [ŋ]. It has an English counterpart /ŋ/ as in finger, sink. The sound is produced in a similar manner in both languages.

B. VOWELS:

The essential problem in teaching native speakers of English to produce the five Spanish vowels is due to the fact that many English vowels are diphthongized. The students will tend to transfer the English diphthongal glide to Spanish. This is partly due to the fact that in English, the lip position for the vowel is formed after the consonant is produced. This results in a glide in the vowel causing the diphthong. In Spanish, the opposite should occur. The lip position of the following vowel is anticipated in the preceding consonant. This principle of vowel anticipation is the major explanation for the presence or absence of diphthongization in Spanish vowels.

/a/ (low central vowel) Although English and Spanish do not have exact corresponding sounds, a close substitute for the Spanish /a/ would be the /a/ from father. This English /a/ is nevertheless somewhat lower.

If the /a/ occurs in an unstressed position, the native speaker of English will tend to transfer the English /ə/ "schwa" used in unstressed syllables.

/e/ (front mid vowel) A close substitute sound in English is the /e/ as in bet. However, in Spanish, the tongue is higher and tenser than in English, and the lips are stretched more tensely. The native speaker of English may tend to diphthongize the /e/ in peso and thus, say /peyso/.

(The difference between the Spanish closed and open /e/ is an allophonic difference.)

/i/ (high front vowel) Although a close substitute sound in English is /i/ of bit, in the production of the Spanish /i/, the tongue is higher and tenser than the English, and the lips are stretched more tensely.

The Spanish /i/, whether in stressed or unstressed syllables, is produced in the same manner. If the /i/ is unstressed in Spanish, the native speaker of English should not transfer the /ə/ "schwa" used in unstressed syllables in English.

/o/ (back mid vowel) An English close substitute is the /ɔ/ in ⟨bought⟩, but the Spanish /o/ is produced by a slightly higher and tenser tongue and rounder lips as in ⟨todo⟩ /todo/.

/u/ (high back vowel) The /u/ of book in English is a close substitute sound. Nevertheless, the Spanish /u/ is produced with a slightly higher and tenser tongue and rounder lips.

Diphthongs:
English vs. Spanish close substitutes:

Diphthong	English	Spanish
/ey/	lay	ley
/ay/	eye	ay
/oy/	boy	voy
/aw/	chow	"chao"

The above English and Spanish diphthongs are all close substitute sounds. The essential difference between the sounds of each pair is simply that the Spanish sound is tenser, and the glide is produced more rapidly.

The Spanish /ey/, /ay/, /oy/ are also somewhat higher than their English counterparts.

C. INTONATION:

Intonation: It is the unit of speech melody in a language that contributes to the total meaning of the utterance. Essential features of intonation are stress, pitch, and juncture.

Stress: English has four stress phonemes (strong ´, weak ˘ secondary ˆ, and tertiary `). Spanish has two principal stress phonemes (strong ´, weak `). The Spanish spoken by a native speaker of English who tends to carry over his four stress patterns into Spanish will have a "sing-song" effect.

Pitch: The basic differences between Spanish and English are that English uses four pitch levels, whereas Spanish uses three (low 1, medium 2, high 3, and English has the extra high pitch 4). Pitch levels that are characteristic of English when carried over to Spanish can give the utterances either a harsh effect or in some cases a completely different meaning.

Juncture: English has three terminal junctures (rising ↑, falling ↓ and sustained /). Spanish also has the same three terminal junctures, but when a falling juncture occurs, the Spanish utterance will end in a much lower pitch than the English utterance.

D. BASIC TYPES OF UTTERANCES

Normal information question:

    English /1211 ↓ /   Spanish /1211 ↓ /

The essential difference which will cause difficulty is that, although the English and Spanish are similar, the English signifies disgust, annoyance or lack of interest.

Example: English: Won't you come on? /1211 ↓ /
        Spanish: ¿Adónde vamos? /1211 ↓ /

Simple statement:
    English /231 ↓ /   Spanish /1211 ↓ /

If the English pattern is carried over to Spanish, the Spanish utterance will sound like an emphatic statement rather than a simple statement.

Example: English: Today is Sunday. /231 ↓ /
        Spanish: Comemos papas. /1211 ↓ /

Question presuming yes-no answer:
    English /233 ↑ /   Spanish /1222 ↑ /

The essential difference between the two languages is the rise. In Spanish, it should be more abrupt than the English, which is a longer rise. The abruptness of the Spanish may seem strange at first to the student, yet this should not make him think that the sentence might be rude or discourteous.

Example: English: He went home? /233 ↑ /
        Spanish: ¿Comiste papas? /1222 ↑ /

Emphatic statement pattern:
    English /241 ↓ /   Spanish /1231 ↓ /

Native speakers of English must try to realize that if the pitch level /3/ in an emphatic statement is said too high, it will become the pitch level /4/ of English and will sound foreign to the native ear.

Example: English: I'm so mad! /241 ↓ /
        Spanish: ¡Estoy furiosa! /1231 ↓ /

Questions presuming an affirmative answer:
    English – – – –   Spanish /1231 | /

The English pattern most closely associated is very rare and, therefore, this pattern can be considered one of the most difficult high-frequency patterns to learn. The Spanish emphatic pattern /1231 ↓ / is the closest to the Spanish pattern used for questions presuming an affirmative answer. The /1231 ↓ / emphatic pattern, however, ends in a sharp drop-off in pitch while the comparable question pattern /1231 | / ends in a sustained terminal juncture (no drop-off in pitch).

II. MORPHOLOGY

A. NOUNS

1. Gender:

Spanish nouns have two genders: masculine and feminine. Principal endings for masculine nouns are: o (muchacho), l (baúl), d (césped), or (pintor), ema problema), ama (drama), and exceptions to the o ending: día, poeta, mapa, clima. Principal endings for feminine nouns: a (niña), ía (tontería), dad (caridad), tad (libertad), ción (acción), ie (serie), umbre (costumbre), and exceptions: mano.

2. Number:

Spanish nouns have two forms: singular and plural. Nouns which end in a consonant form the plural by adding the plural allomorph {es}. Nouns ending in a vowel add the plural allomorph {s}.

3. Implications:

Native speakers of English may tend to carry over into Spanish some of the phonetic habits to which they have become accustomed. The unvoiced plural allomorph {s} following a noun ending in a vowel may be incorrectly pronounced (example: años [añoz] instead of /años/ due to the normal pronunciation /ɨz/ or /z/ corresponding to ⟨es⟩ or ⟨s⟩ in final position in English:

Example: ⟨he has⟩   /hi haz/

B. NOUN MARKERS OR DETERMINATIVES

Some noun markers in English distinguish number, but in no case do they distinguish gender. In Spanish, noun markers do distinguish number in all cases, but the Spanish differs from the English in that the majority of its noun markers distinguish gender. (Exceptions: mi, tu, su.) The speaker of English must accustom himself to the masculine/feminine contrast in both singular and plural numbers.

Singular		Plural	
Masculine	Feminine	Masculine	Feminine
un	una	unos	unas
el	la	los	las
este	esta	estos	estas
ese	esa	esos	esas
aquel	aquella	aquellos	aquellas
nuestro	nuestra	nuestros	nuestras
vuestro	vuestra	vuestros	vuestras
mi		mis	
tu		tus	
su		sus	

The above table lists articles, demonstrative adjectives, and possessive adjectives. The articles can be considered the primary determiners whereas the adjectives, demonstrative and possessive, can be considered the subclasses of the primary determiners.

One must keep in mind that only one determiner can appear in a simple noun phrase: (D + N).

C. PRONOUNS

1. Personal Pronouns

a. *Subject Pronouns:* Although there is no clear-cut point of interference, the subject pronouns in Spanish do differ somewhat in their use from those in English. Subject pronouns in Spanish are generally used for purposes of emphasis or contrast in either declarative or interrogative statements. In any other case, the subject pronoun is omitted; the verb ending indicating the doer of the action is sufficient.

The second person singular and plural, formal and informal, in English is indicated by one word ⟨you⟩. In Spanish, there are distinct subject pronoun forms which are conjugated with different forms of the verb as can be seen in the chart below.

2ND PERSON FORMS: SPANISH

		Verb agreement	Example
Singular	Formal: usted Informal: tú	3rd singular 2nd singular	usted camina tú caminas
Plural	Formal: ustedes Informal: vosotros	3rd plural 2nd plural	ustedes caminan vosotros camináis

b. *Direct Object Pronouns: conjunctive pronouns:* The following chart illustrates that, in some cases, a one-to-one correspondence between Spanish and English does not exist, thus causing a problem for the native speaker of English learning Spanish.

English	Spanish
me	me
you	te, le or lo, la
him	le, lo
her	la
it (m)	lo
it (f)	la
us	nos
you	os, les or los, las
them (m)	les, los
them (f)	las
them (m) (inanimate)	los
them (f) (inanimate)	las

The third person singular ⟨him⟩ has two counterparts which are interchangeable. ⟨Le⟩ is more commonly used in Spain, whereas ⟨lo⟩ is more frequently used in Latin America. The same principle applies to ⟨them⟩ (masc.). ⟨Les⟩ is more commonly used in Spain, ⟨los⟩ is more often heard in Latin America, and they are interchangeable.

The essential problem is the correspondence between ⟨you⟩ in English and its various Spanish counterparts. The Spanish form for ⟨you⟩ can be singular informal ⟨te⟩ or formal ⟨le⟩ which is interchangeable with ⟨lo⟩ and ⟨la⟩. The formal ⟨le⟩ does not indicate gender as do ⟨lo⟩

⟨la⟩ and is more commonly used in Spain, whereas ⟨lo⟩ and ⟨la⟩ are more frequently used in Latin America. The plural formal and informal follow the same pattern. ⟨Os⟩ is the informal: ⟨les⟩ is the formal second person more commonly used in Spain and unmarked for gender whereas ⟨los⟩ ⟨las⟩, characteristic of Latin American Spanish, are inflected for gender.

   c. *Indirect Object Pronouns: conjunctive pronouns:* The indirect object pronouns present a similar problem of correspondence, as can be demonstrated according to the following chart:

English	Spanish
me	me
you	te, le, (se + direct object)
him	le, (se + direct object)
her	le, (se + direct object)
us	nos
you	os, les, (se + direct object)
them (m)	les, (se + direct object)
them (f)	les, (se + direct object)

There is only one Spanish form corresponding to each of the following English indirect objects: him, her, them (m), them (f), except if the indirect object is followed by a direct object. In this case, the indirect object ⟨le, les⟩ changes to ⟨se⟩.

   The only other possible difficulty which arises concerns the two forms of the second person singular: the formal ⟨le⟩ and the informal ⟨te⟩. The native speaker of English must accustom himself to the formal ⟨le⟩ and the informal ⟨te⟩ pronouns corresponding to the English ⟨you⟩. It will then be easier to understand that:

   a) ⟨le⟩ when followed by a direct object changes to ⟨se⟩
   b) ⟨te⟩ when followed by a direct object remains the same.*

---

*Note: The position of direct and indirect object pronouns in Spanish will be discussed in the section dealing with syntax.

d) *Reflexive Pronouns* (see reflexive verbs)

e) *Prepositional Personal Pronouns: disjunctive pronouns:* Spanish and English forms both follow their own regular pattern:

Spanish: preposition & subject pronoun

Exception: 1st singular ⟨mí⟩

2nd singular ⟨tí⟩

English: preposition + object pronoun

The possible area of interference deals only with the first and second person singular in Spanish, whose forms do not follow the regular pattern:

⟨con⟩ + subject pronoun

conmigo — with me

contigo — with you (informal singular)

consigo — with himself, herself.

2. Relative Pronouns

The English relative pronouns are not inflected for either gender or number whereas in Spanish, certain relative pronouns are inflected for gender, others for number, and others for both. The following chart indicates how Spanish pronouns are inflected.

	Gender	Number	English
Que	—	—	who, what
Quien	—	X	whom, who
Cual	—	X	which
Cuyo	X	X	whose

3. Interrogative Pronouns

The difficulty which native speakers of English experience when using the Spanish relative pronouns also occurs with the interrogative pronouns. The following chart indicates how Spanish interrogative pronouns are inflected.

	Gender	Number	English
Qué	—	—	what
Quién	—	X	who, whom
Cuál	—	X	which

D. ADJECTIVES

1. Agreement

In Spanish, nouns and adjectives agree in gender and number whereas in English this agreement does not exist. To solve this, native speakers of English can learn two major classes of adjectives: a) adjectives whose endings distinguish gender by their ending, and b) adjectives whose endings are unrelated to gender distinction.

Class a) includes the majority of Spanish adjectives:
1) those which follow the most common pattern:

ENDINGS	Singular	Plural
Masculine	o	os
Feminine	a	as

This characteristic is common to both nouns and adjectives.
Example:

NOUN	Singular	Plural
Masculine	negro	negros
Feminine	negra	negras
ADJECTIVE		
Masculine	chico	chicos
Feminine	chica	chicas

2) those denoting nationality: The feminine form adds a to the base form replacing the masculine singular o or ø; the feminine plural is based on the feminine singular.
Example:

	Singular	Plural
Masculine	francés	franceses
Feminine	francesa	francesas

3) those ending in ⟨on⟩, ⟨an⟩ and ⟨or⟩: These follow the pattern of adjectives which denote nationality.
4) articles
5) demonstratives

Class b) includes:

1) adjectives whose masculine singular forms do not end in /o/ and/or have no distinguishing forms regarding gender: examples: verde, inteligente, débil, azul, marrón, gris, escolar, capaz, febril. (No attempt at completeness) This characteristic is also common to both nouns and adjectives.
Example:

	Singular	Plural
Noun Adjective	fuente inteligente	fuentes inteligentes
Noun Adjective	ferrocarril débil	ferrocarriles débiles
Noun Adjective	rapaz capaz	rapaces capaces

2. Apocopation

In Spanish, certain adjectives have shortened forms losing the final vowel or syllable when used before the noun (unstressed position). These adjectives can be classified according to the different forms of apocopation:

a) When placed before the noun, the following adjectives lose the final /o/, but when placed after the noun, they retain it:

algún — alguno
buen — bueno
mal — malo
ningún — ninguno
primer — primero

b) When placed before the noun, the following adjective loses the final syllable, but when placed after the noun, it retains it: gran — grande.

The position of the above adjectives is interchangeable

in identical constructions, but it must be kept in mind that gran – grande, changes in lexical meaning. Gran refers to the virtue of magnanimity or to renown; grande refers to physical size.)

    c) The following adjectives are also apocopated according to the above rules, but they are not interchangeable in identical constructions:

> un – uno (rule a)
> tercer – tercero (rule a)
> cien – ciento (rule b)

    d) *Ciento* is shortened to *cien* before plural nouns and before a number larger than itself.

    e) Preceding the name of a masculine saint, *santo* becomes *san*. Exception: names beginning with /do/ or /to/ as in Santo Domingo, Santo Tomás.

E. VERBS

1. *Regular Verbs*

In English, with few exceptions, verbs are inflected for mood and tense but generally not for person and number. Example: 3rd person singular, present tense. The native speaker of English must accustom himself to the Spanish verbs which are inflected for mood, tense, person, and number. Using the infinitive as a base form, the regular verbs in Spanish can be categorized into three verb classes according to their infinitive endings: /ar/, /er/, /ir/. With two exceptions, the endings of the /er/ and /ir/ verbs are the same in all tenses and moods:

    a) *Present tense:* 1st and 2nd persons plural
    Example:

	1st person plural	2nd person plural
er verb ir verb	comemos vivimos	coméis vivís

    b) *Imperative mood:* 2nd person plural informal
    Example:

er ir	comed vivid

Verbs in English have no clear-cut categorization into conjugations nor are there "vowel markers" preceding the endings of each conjugation as in Spanish. In Spanish, the /ar/ verbs are easily distinguished by the characteristic vowel /a/, whereas /e/ denotes the /er/ verbs and /i/ the /ir/ verbs.

Due to the inflection, the regular verb system in Spanish has recurring person-number indicators in all tenses except the preterite.

	Singular	Plural
1st person	∅	mos
2nd person	s	is
3rd person	∅	n

Also characteristic of Spanish tenses is a set of mood and tense markers. These mood and tense markers immediately precede the person-number indicators in the formation of the conjugated verb. Example:

com	ería	mos
stem	mood and tense marker	person-number indicator

CHART OF MOOD AND TENSE MARKERS *

Indicative	Present	a	e ⟶	
	Imperfect	aba	ia ⟶	
	Future	ará	erá	irá
Subjunctive	Present	e	a ⟶	
	Imperfect	(ara)	(iera) ⟶	
		(ase)	(iese) ⟶	
Conditional	Simple conditional	aría	ería	iría

*Chart adapted from Cárdenas, p. 34 and also Politzer and Staubach, p. 111.

Imperative mood of regular verbs

There are five Spanish imperative forms which are as follows:

2nd person formal: singular—plural

2nd person informal: singular—plural

1st person: plural

2nd person formal (usted) (ustedes)

Singular: formed by using the third person singular subjunctive

Example: Hable usted más lentamente, por favor.

Plural: formed by using the third person plural subjunctive

Example: Hablen ustedes más lentamente, por favor.

2nd person informal (tú) (vosotros)

Singular: formed by using the third person singular indicative

Example: Habla más lento.

Plural: (used very infrequently in Spanish America) formed by using infinitive and taking off the /r/ and adding /d/.

Example: habla|r = hablad

come|r = comed

vivi|r = vivid

1st person (nosotros)

Plural: formed by using the first person plural subjunctive:

Example: Hablemos más lentamente.

2. Irregular Verbs

The following section has been adapted from Politzer, Robert L. and Charles N. Staubach; *Teaching Spanish, A Linguistic Orientation;* New York, 1965, p. 115; charts pp. 116–117.

Verbs which are "unclassable" are those which do not fall into any of the regular conjugational patterns. Nevertheless, certain recurring patterns among these verbs show uniformity. The above mentioned chart should be used for reference.

Present indicative
All verbs have:
1) same stem-ending arrangement in:
   a) 2nd person singular (sabe|s, puede|s)
   b) 3rd person singular (sabe, puede)
   c) 3rd person plural (sabe|n, puede|n)
2) regular stem and ending in:
   a) 1st person plural (sabe|mos, pode|mos)
   b) 2nd person plural (sabé|is, podé|is)
   Exceptions: SER, IR and HABER

Imperfect Indicative
1) All verbs "regular": sabíamos, podíamos
2) Exceptions: ser, ir and haber. However, these three verbs follow the same pattern on an irregular stem.

> era, eras, era, etc.
> iba, ibas, iba, etc.
> había, habías, había, etc.

Future and conditional
There is one set of endings for each of these two tenses. The only irregularity to be learned is the stem.
> Example: *Future:* sabré, sabrás, sabrá, etc.
> *Conditional:* sabría, sabrías, sabría, etc.

Preterite
Irregular verbs follow two patterns in the preterite tense:
1) Verbs with unstressed ending in the first person singular (key form), follow the same "strong" pattern. Example: supe, supiste, supo, etc.; pude, pudiste, pudo, etc.
   > Exceptions: dijeron, trajeron, hizo,—dujeron (as in condujeron)
2) Verbs with stressed ending (dí, salí) follow the regular pattern of the 2nd and 3rd verb conjugations—í, -íste, -ió, etc.
   > Example: di, diste, dió, etc.; salí, saliste, salió, etc.
   > Exceptions: cayó, cayeron; oyó, oyeron
3) Exceptions to these patterns: SER, IR

Present subjunctive
   1) Present subjunctive stem is the same in all persons in all the "unclassable" irregular verbs. Subjunctive formation of stem is based on first person singular present indicative.
      Example:

	Indicative	Subjunctive
1st sing.	dig*o* pong*o*	dig*a* pong*a*

   2) Exceptions to this rule: poder and querer which follow Class 1, radical changing verbs.
   3) Other exceptions: ser, ir, haber, saber, estar, dar
Imperfect subjunctive
All verbs follow the same pattern: regular imperfect subjunctive endings replace the third person plural ending of the preterite — ron.
   Example: salieron → saliera
            dijeron → dijera
Singular imperative informal: (tú)
It is based on the third person singular present indicative.
   Example: saber → él sabe → sabe
                traer → él trae → trae
   Exceptions: ser, ir, haber, tener, poder, hacer, venir, decir, oír, salir, valer
Plural imperative informal: (vosotros)
Its formation is always based on the infinitive.
   Example: saber → sabed
            tener → tened
            ir → id

3. Radical Changing Verbs

In Spanish, this class of verbs is labeled radical changing because the "radical" vowel (often referred to as "stem" vowel or "root" vowel) changes.

The following are the three classes of radical changing verbs:

CLASS I

Conjugation involved: first /ar/ and second /er/ conjugations.

Change involved: when stressed, the radical vowel /e/ changes to /ie/ and the radical vowel /o/ changes to /we/.

Tenses and moods involved:

1) Present indicative: all singular and 3rd plural
   Example: pensar to pienso, etc.
           volver to vuelvo, etc.
2) Present subjunctive: all singular and 3rd plural
   Example: pensar to piensas, etc.
           volver to vuelva, etc.
3) Singular imperative informal:
   Example: pensar to piensa
           volver to vuelve

CLASS II

Conjugation involved: third /ir/ conjugation.

Change involved: when stressed, stem vowel /e/ changes to /ie/ and the stem vowel /o/ changes to /we/; if ending is stressed, stem vowel /e/ changes to /i/ and stem vowel /o/ changes to /u/, unless the ending contains stressed /i/.

Tenses and moods involved:

1. Stem vowel stressed:

Tense	Persons	E changes to IE Example: sentir	O changes to UE Example: dormir
Present indicative	sing. 1, 2, 3	siento, sientes, siente	duermo, duermes, duerme
	plu. 3	sienten	duermen
Present subjunctive	sing. 1, 2, 3	sienta, sientas, sienta	duerma, duermas, duerma
	plu. 3	sientan	duerman
Imperative sing.; formal, inf. plu.; formal		sienta, siente sientan	duerma, duerme duerman

2. Ending stressed:

Tense	Persons	E changes to I Example: sentir	O changes to U Example: dormir
Preterite	sing. 3 plu. 3	sintió sintieron	durmió durmieron
Present subjunctive	plu. 1, 2	sintamos, sintáis	durmamos, durmáis
Imperfect—era Subjunctive—ese	All	sintiera, etc. sintiese, etc.	durmiera, etc. durmiese, etc.
Present participle		sintiendo	durmiendo

CLASS III

Conjugation involved: third /ir/ conjugation.

Change involved: when stressed, the radical vowel /e/ changes to /i/; if ending is stressed, the radical vowel /e/ also changes to /i/, in certain cases.

Tense and moods involved:

1) Stem vowel stressed: tenses and moods involved are the same as comparable category in Class II. Example: pedir.
2) Ending stressed: tenses and moods involved are the same as comparable category in Class II. Example: pedir.

4. Orthographic changing verbs

Orthographic changing verbs are those which present certain regular spelling changes in order to preserve regular sound-spelling relationship throughout the paradigm. The following are classifications for these verbs:

1) *Verbs involved: verbs ending in* ⟨-car⟩ *and* ⟨-gar⟩.

   Example: buscar, llegar

   Change involved: these verbs change

   ⟨c⟩ to ⟨qu⟩ and

   ⟨g⟩ to ⟨gu⟩.

   Tenses and moods involved:

   preterite: first person singular

   present subjunctive: all

2) *Verbs involved:* verbs ending in ⟨-guar⟩.
   Example: averiguar
   Change involved: ⟨gu⟩ changes to ⟨gü⟩ before ⟨e⟩.
   Tenses and moods involved: same as in 1.
3) *Verbs involved:* verbs ending in ⟨-zar⟩.
   Example: empezar
   Changes involved: ⟨z⟩ changes to ⟨c⟩ before ⟨e⟩.
   Tenses and moods involved: same as in 1. The above change, found almost everywhere in Spanish, is conventional rather than essential; nevertheless, it remains in the category of orthographic changing verbs.
4) *Verbs involved:* verbs ending in ⟨-cer⟩ or ⟨-cir⟩.
   Example: convencer
   Change involved: ⟨c⟩ changes to ⟨z⟩ before ⟨a⟩ and ⟨o⟩.
   Tenses and moods involved:
   present indicative: first person singular
   present subjunctive: all.
5) *Verbs involved:* verbs ending in ⟨-ger⟩ and ⟨-gir⟩.
   Example: dirigir
   Change involved: ⟨g⟩ changes to ⟨j⟩ before ⟨a⟩ and ⟨o⟩.
   Tenses and moods involved: same as 4.
6) *Verbs involved:* verbs ending in ⟨-guir⟩.
   Example: seguir
   Change involved: ⟨gu⟩ changes to ⟨g⟩ before ⟨a⟩ and ⟨o⟩.
   Tenses and moods involved: same as in 4.
7) *Verbs involved:* verbs ending in ⟨-ecer, -ocer, -ucir⟩.
   Example: conocer
   Change involved: insertion of ⟨z⟩ before ⟨c⟩.
   Tenses and moods involved:
   present indicative: first person singular
   present subjunctive: all

Class 7 presents a change in the first person singular, indicative and subjunctive, which is partly related to orthographic changing verbs but which is also an irregularity.

In these forms, ⟨conozco, conozca⟩ /konoško, konoška/ the insertion of the ⟨z⟩ before ⟨c⟩ /š before k/ is a purely orthographic change. However, in the 1st person singular indicative and present subjunctive, the /k/ is a genuine morphological irregularity.

5. Reflexive Verbs

There is a similarity in the formation of the reflexive in English and in Spanish. In English, the reflexive verb is formed as follows: Subject pronoun – verb – reflexive pronoun. The Spanish formation of the reflexive verb differs slightly. Subject pronoun* – reflexive pronoun – verb.

In Spanish, the verb itself follows the regular conjugational pattern.

Example:

Subject Pronoun	Reflexive Pronoun	Verb
(yo)	me	levanto
(tú)	te	levantas
(él)	se	levanta
(nosotros)	nos	levantamos
(vosotros)	os	levantáis
(ellos)	se	levantan

Note: See position of reflexive pronoun in syntax section.

The reflexive verb is conjugated in all tenses in exactly the same manner as the non-reflexive verb and follows the previously outlined word order: (subject pronoun)-reflexive pronoun-verb.

Examples: imperfect: (yo) me levantaba
future: (yo) me levantaré
preterite: (yo) me levanté
present perfect: (yo) me he levantado
pluperfect: (yo) me había levantado
future perfect: (yo) me habré levantado

---

* It is well to note that the use of the subject pronoun in the reflexive verb construction in Spanish is not only optional but also very infrequently used.

The imperative of the reflexive form is also formed in exactly the same manner as the non-reflexive verbs and adds the reflexive pronoun to the verb form.

Examples:

levánta	te	=	levántate
informal singular imperative verb form	˙ reflexive pronoun		informal singular imperative

levánte	se	=	levántese
formal singular imperative verb form	reflexive pronoun		formal singular imperative

levanta	os	=	levantaos
informal plural imperative	reflexive pronoun		informal plural imperative

Exception: for the second person plural imperative of the reflexive verb the /d/ is dropped.

levánten	se	=	levántense
formal plural imperative	reflexive pronoun		formal plural imperative

levantémo	nos	=	levantémonos
first person plural imperative	reflexive pronoun		first person plural imperative

III. SYNTAX

SPANISH VERB TENSES

	Indicative Mood	Subjunctive Mood	Imperative Mood	Conditional Mood
Simple	Present Imperfect Future Preterite	Present Imperfect	1 command form for each of: Informal (tú; vosotros) Formal (usted; ustedes) Let's	Present
Complex	Present Perfect Pluperfect Future Perfect	Present Perfect Pluperfect		Past

III. SYNTAX

A. VERB TENSES AND MOODS

The verb is characterized by different tenses or moods. Tenses denote time distinctions whereas moods denote the manner in which the action is conceived, either as a fact, a possibility, a command, or a condition. Formal analysis shows that the Spanish verb system is composed of four moods: indicative, subjunctive, conditional, imperative; and with the exception of the latter, each mood includes various tenses. The similarities and differences of the English and Spanish verb systems are reviewed below.

Both in English and in Spanish, the indicative mood represents the denoted action as an objective fact. The indicative mood in Spanish consists of seven tenses; four simple and three complex. The four simple tenses are: present, imperfect, future and preterite; the three complex are: present perfect, pluperfect and future perfect.

1. *Indicative Mood: simple tenses*

Present tense

Spanish uses the present tense to describe an event which is in progress at the moment of speaking or a state of being. In addition, Spanish uses the present tense to express the following:

    a) an event or state which began in the past and continues into the present.

    Examples:

        ¿Desde cuándo *estás* en los Estados Unidos?

        ¿Cuánto tiempo hace que *estás* en los Estados Unidos?

        Hace tres meses que estoy en los Estados Unidos.

The present tense in these cases is signaled by the use of the adverbial expressions desde cuándo, cuánto tiempo hace. However, in English, these corresponding adverbs would be used with the past progressive or past perfect tenses.

Imperfect tense

English has no such comparable tense but the use of the auxiliary ⟨used to⟩ or ⟨was + ing⟩ may signal a similar verb function. The imperfect tense in Spanish is used to express:

a) a continuing past event or state, the beginning or end of which is not relevant.

Example: Mi hermana *cosía* el vestido. Hacía frío.

b) a customary, repeated or habitual past action.

Example: Yo *caminaba* a la escuela cuando tenía nueve años. Me *levantaba* a las ocho.

c) telling time in the past.

Example: *Eran* las ocho cuando llegó. Or age in the past.

Example: Yo caminaba a la escuela cuando *tenía* nueve años.

d) indirect discourse.

Example: Dijo que *venía*.

(see imperfect-preterite contrast)

Future

Both English and Spanish use the future tense to refer to an event or state which has not taken place at the time of the utterance.

In addition, Spanish uses the future tense to express probability — but in reference to present time.

Example:

Present tense	Future tense (expressing probability in reference to present time)
Probablemente *son* las tres.	*Serán* las tres.
Probablemente *está* en casa.	*Estará* en casa.

Preterite

The preterite tense in Spanish is used to express an event or state which is viewed as completed at some point in the past.

Example: *Almorcé* a las cinco.

El señor *llegó* a la casa con unos paquetes.

The English tense usually used to express the same type of event or state is the simple past. (I walked, I bought, etc.). There is, however, no one-to-one correspondence between these two tenses. The English simple past can also denote repeated, customary action:

Example: Ayer *fui* a la tienda. Yesterday I went to the store.

El año pasado *iba* a la tienda. Last year I went to the store.
I used to go to the store.

Preterite — Imperfect contrast

Both tenses may be found in the same utterances describing differences between two events in the past.

a) the imperfect is used quite often to express a continuing action in the past. If, at a particular point within the duration of the imperfect action, another action has been completed, then the preterite tense is used to describe the completed action.

Example: María hacía la cena cuando llegó su marido del trabajo.

b) certain verbs change lexical meaning due to the difference of tense.

Lo supe esta mañana. → I found out this morning.
Lo sabía. ——————→ I knew it.

Conocí a la Sra. Escobedo. ——————→ I met Mrs. Escobedo.
Conocía a la Sra. Escobedo. ——————→ I knew Mrs. Escobedo.

No quiso ir. ——————→ He refused to go.
No quería ir. ——————→ He didn't want to go.

Quiso ir. ——————→ He intended to go.
Quería ir. ——————→ He wanted to go.

Pudo ir. ——————→ He managed to go.
No podía ir. ——————→ He couldn't (wasn't able) to go.

c) the imperfect tense may be used two or more times in the same sentence if the events occurred simultaneously according to the aforementioned uses of the imperfect tense.

Example: Siempre leía el periódico cuando desayunaba.

d) the preterite tense may be used two or more times in the same sentence if the events occurred according to the aforementioned uses of the preterite tense.

Example: Compré la langosta y la cociné para la cena.

Indicative Mood: compound tenses

Present perfect

Like the preterite, the present perfect tense in Spanish is used to express a completed action. But the essential difference between the two tenses is that the present perfect is used to express a finished action with reference to the present. It is normally used as the present perfect is in English and corresponds to the English: have + past participle.

Example: José Manuel ha estado en España.

José Manuel has been in Spain.

España ha producido grandes figuras literarias.

Spain has produced famous literary figures.

The present perfect may also be replaced by the preterite especially after ⟨ya⟩.

Example: Ya lo he hecho ⟶ Ya lo hice.

Pluperfect

The pluperfect tense in Spanish is used to express an event in the past but which has occurred before another past event (expressed or implied). It corresponds to the English: had + past participle and is used in the same manner. (However, refer to conditional clauses for use of pluperfect subjunctive.)

Example: Ya le había dicho que sí.

I had already said yes.

Dijo que no lo había hecho.

He said he had not done it.

Future perfect

The future perfect tense in Spanish corresponds to the same tense in English: shall (will) have + past participle. It is used in the same manner, to express a future event or state which will take place before another future event or state is completed.

> Example:
> > Para cuando llegues, habré terminado esta carta.
> > > By the time you arrive, I shall have finished writing this letter.

2. Subjunctive Mood

The subjunctive mood in Spanish carries with it a subjective attitude on the part of the speaker as opposed to an objective fact expressed by the indicative mood. The subjunctive mood in English is much less frequently used than in Spanish and a comparison of the English subjunctive with the Spanish subjunctive would not be particularly profitable. The subjunctive mood in Spanish consists of four tenses: two simple and two complex. The simple tenses are the present and the imperfect tenses in two forms; the complex are the present perfect and the pluperfect tenses. In general, the use and sequence of tenses is as in English.

Present subjunctive

The present subjunctive in Spanish can indicate either a present or future event which is not an objective fact but rather a thought or feeling in the mind of the speaker. The present subjunctive will generally follow a principal verb either in the present or future tense.

> Example: Espero que venga.
> > Insistiré en que venga.

Imperfect subjunctive

The imperfect subjunctive can indicate any tense in the past. The event indicated in the subjunctive is not an objective fact but rather a thought or feeling in the mind of the speaker. It is generally used after a past tense in the indicative.

> Example: Insistía en que viniera.
> > Mandó que se hiciera.

Present perfect subjunctive and pluperfect subjunctive

The present perfect and pluperfect subjunctive refer, just as their counterparts in the indicative mood, to completed actions in the past and to actions which occurred before other events in the past. However, the subjunctive mood carries with it the subjective attitude on the part of the speaker for each of these tenses.

> Example: Tenía miedo de que lo hubieran descubierto.
>
> Espera que haya aprobado la materia.

Use of the subjunctive:

The subjunctive mood is used in noun, adjectival and adverbial clauses as follows:

Noun clauses

    a) The subjunctive mood is used in the dependent clause which follows verbs or phrases of emotion, doubt, forbidding, desire, denial, and command. Example:

emotion	⟶	Siento que te hayas caído.
doubt	⟶	Dudo que venga.
forbidding	⟶	No permito que vayas.
desire	⟶	Quiero que venga.
denial	⟶	Niega que lo haya escrito.
command	⟶	¡He dicho que vayas!

    b) The subjunctive is also used in noun clauses after impersonal expressions.

> Example: Es un milagro que lo haya hecho.
>
> Parece mentira que quiera venir.

Adjective clauses

    a) The subjunctive is used in an adjectival clause if the antecedent which the clause modifies is either non-existent or indefinite.

> Example: Busco a un muchacho que me quiera ayudar.
>
> No he encontrado a nadie que me pueda ayudar.

    b) The subjunctive is sometimes used after a superlative expression implying opinion rather than fact on the part of the speaker.

Example: Esa es la película más tonta que jamás se haya producido.

Adverbial clauses

a) The subjunctive is used after conjunctions denoting purpose, unaccomplished result, proviso, supposition, exception, etc.

Example: purpose ──────────→ para que

unaccomplished result─→ de manera que

proviso───────────→ con tal que

supposition ─────────→ supuesto que

exception───────────→ sin que

b) The subjunctive is used in temporal clauses where futurity is implied.

Example:

*Cuando llegue mi hermana tendré que arreglar la habitación.

Antes de que se me olvide le quiero decir a Mariana que pase por acá.

Example:

actual present: Te engañas cuando piensas que eres inteligente.

historical present: Cuando llegan los Moros a Asturias son rechazados por Pelayo.

habitual present: Cuando llueve me quedo en casa.

c) The subjunctive is used after indefinite expressions such as:

cualquier, cualquiera	comoquiera que
por + adj + que	cuandoquiera que
por + adv + que	dondequiera que
por menos que	quienquiera que
por poco que	
por más que	
por mucho que	

3. *Conditional Mood*

The conditional mood expresses an idea which is not a reality but rather a possibility. It has two tenses: the

---

* Cuando may also be followed by the present indicative if the present is actual, historical, or habitual.

simple and the past conditional. The simple conditional has often been described as a past tense with reference to the future. The uses of the simple and the past conditional in Spanish are essentially the same as those in English.

a) In both Spanish and English, the simple conditional tense can be used to note willingness or desire.

Me dijo que trataría de ir al cine.

b) 1) The simple conditional tense is used in "softened" statements to give a less dogmatic tone to statements denoting obligation.

Usted debería escribirlo ahora.

2) The simple conditional tense is also used in "softened" statements to indicate courtesy or consideration.

¿Podría usted venir a mi casa mañana?

¿Me podría explicar el problema?

3) The verbs ⟨desear⟩ and ⟨querer⟩ are interchangeable with ⟨gustar⟩ where used with the simple conditional tense in "softened" statements.

A ella le gustaría comprar un vestido.

Desearía comprar un vestido.

⎡The verb ⟨querer⟩ is also used with the imper-⎤
⎢fect subjunctive to indicate politeness.　　　　⎥
⎣　¿Quisiera usted tomar una taza de café?　　　⎦

c) The simple conditional tense in Spanish is often used in main clauses corresponding to the English could, would, or should.

Él podría salir bien en los exámenes.

He could do well on the examinations.

Él diría que sí.

He would say yes.

d) Perhaps the principal use of the simple conditional tense is to denote an unlikely or contrary-to-fact event. The following is the sequence of tenses for ⟨si⟩ clauses in Spanish:

1) In neutral ⟨si⟩ clauses, the present indicative is used.

Si vienes mañana iremos al teatro.

Si llueve no voy.

2) Contrary-to-fact ⟨si⟩ clauses denote a situation which is unlikely to be fulfilled (unreal). Some of these conditions are referent to the present, others to the past (c).

The imperfect subjunctive is used in ⟨si⟩ clauses which refer to the present.

Si lo quisiera comer, lo ordenaría.

If I wanted to eat it, I would order it.

The implication is that I don't like it, so, I won't order it. It is, therefore, unlikely that the condition will be fulfilled.

3) Contrary-to-fact ⟨si⟩ clauses can also refer to the past. The pluperfect subjunctive is then used in the ⟨si⟩ clause.

Si (él) hubiera (hubiese) llegado, (yo) habría ido.

or

Si hubiera (hubiese) llegado, hubiera ido.

If he had come, I would have gone.

The implication is that since "he" did not come, "I" did not go anywhere. The condition is not fulfilled.

4) The time element with the use of the past conditional tense may depart from the above sequence as illustrated by the following examples:

Si no fuera por el señor pedante, Roberto los hubiera (habría) invitado.

Si me hubiera devuelto los otros préstamos, con mucho gusto le daría más dinero.

4. *Imperative Mood*

The imperative mood in both Spanish and English is used to express a command or an order. There are five Spanish imperative forms, which are as follows:

2nd person formal: singular — plural

2nd person informal: singular — plural

1st person: — plural

Examples: Recoge la ropa que has dejado tirada.
　　　　　Pick up the clothes which you've left.
　　　　　Ven a comer.
　　　　　Come eat.

B. SYNTACTICAL PATTERNS

Articles

1 and 2. *Uses of the definite and indefinite article:*

Although the basic uses for the definite and indefinite article are the same in both Spanish and English, there are nevertheless occasions where there is a lack of correspondence between the two languages. This lack of correspondence will be discussed in two sections:

　A. Spanish omits it where English uses it.
　B. Spanish uses it where English omits it.

A. *Spanish omits the article where English uses it in the following cases:*

　1) a noun in apposition not being used for purpose of identification

　　　Roma, sede del Santo Imperio Romano, es una ciudad caracterizada por la historia y la belleza.

　　If is is used for identification, the article is maintained

　　　Franco, el caudillo de España, ...

　2) before a numeral which modifies a title

　　　Carlos Quinto del Imperio Romano era Carlos Primero de España.

　3) in enumerations

　　　Madre e hija suelen hacer los bordados para el ajuar.

　4) neither the definite nor the indefinite article is employed at the head of printed titles of books and articles

　　　Historia de España　　The History of Spain
　　　Texto de Lecturas　　A Text of Basic Readings
　　　Básicas

　5) a noun following ⟨sin⟩ usually does not use an article; this form may correspond to English noun + less

El hombre sin sombrero...
The man without a hat...
Un mantel sin mancha...
A spotless tablecloth...

6) a noun following ⟨ser⟩ in an impersonal construction
Es mentira.   It's a lie.

7) a noun used in an indeterminate sense with a verb expressing a concrete idea
No tengo tiempo para hacerlo.
I haven't got the time to do it.

8) when a noun is employed as an adjective to speak of the subject's quality or character, profession, rank, nationality, political affiliation, sex, etc.
Soy ingeniero y soldado.
I am an engineer and a soldier.
Él es profesor.
He is a professor.
¿Es sastre su hermano?
Is your brother a tailor?

9) before a noun in apposition
Austria, país pintoresco, ofrece un panorama único.
Austria, a picturesque country,...

10) with certain indefinite words or expressions
before: otro, cierto, ciento, mil
after: tal, semejante, tan + adj. + noun, como, de, que

B. *Spanish uses the article where English does not in the following cases:*

1) with abstract nouns; with nouns used in a general sense
—abstract noun: La lealtad es una de las virtudes más apreciadas por el hombre. Loyalty is one of the virtues most revered by man.
—noun used in a general sense especially as representative of an entire class or species to which it belongs:

La naranja es producto de las huertas valen-
cianas.

Oranges are a product of the orchards of
Valencia.

2) with proper nouns
   —before descriptive titles when these are not used
   in direct address (exceptions: sor, fray, santo)
   > El Presidente Alessandri fue un chileno muy
   > famoso.
   > President Alessandri was a very famous Chilean.
   —when used to denote one's work, writings, etc.,
   the proper noun may also use the definite article
   > ¿Tienes un ejemplar del Quijote?
   > Have you got a copy of Don Quijote?

3) with geographical names when modified
   > En la España del Siglo de Oro floreció la li-
   > teratura.
   > Literature flourished during Spain's Golden
   > Age.

4) with names of certain countries and cities (usage
   varies)
   > el Canadá,   la Florida,   el Brasil,   el Perú,
   > el Japón,   la Mancha (province of Spain)
   Note: Some names include the article as part of the
   name itself: La Coruña, La Paz, La Habana.

5) the definite article is used in Spanish to refer to the
   parts of the body whereas the possessive pronoun
   is used in English
   > Tengo la cara sucia.
   > My face is dirty.
   > Tiene los dientes preciosos.
   > Her teeth are beautiful.

6) with adjectives of nationality denoting languages
   the definite article is used *except* in the following
   instances:
   —after preposition ⟨en⟩
   —some expressions formed with ⟨de⟩
   —immediately following hablar

—some speakers would use the article after: apren-
der, enseñar, escribir, estudiar (usage varies)

Example: El francés, el español y el italiano son
idiomas románicos.

7) the definite article is used with
   —names of seasons
   En la primavera salen las flores.
   Flowers bloom in spring.
   —days of the week when meaning denoted is "on
   Monday"
   Exception: dating letters
   La ganga empezó el sábado.
   The sale began on Saturday.
   Los lunes voy al médico.
   I go to the doctor's on Mondays.
   —hours of the day
   Son las tres de la tarde.
   It's three P.M.
   —time expressions when modified by próximo,
   pasado, etc.
   El lunes próximo vendré a verte.
   I'll come to see you next Monday.
   —names of months may use the article, but only
   when modified (usage varies)
   El pasado junio fui a París.
   I went to Paris last June.

8) a noun in apposition with nosotros, vosotros, ustedes
   will use the definite article
   Vosotros los asturianos coméis fabada.

9) the definite article may be used before verbs acting
   as nouns, especially when these are subjects of the
   sentence
   El poder dominar varios idiomas es un don espe-
   cial.
   The ability to master several foreign languages
   requires a special talent.

10) before the four cardinal points
    el sur ⟶ south   el norte ⟶ north

el este $\longrightarrow$ east el oeste $\longrightarrow$ west
11) before many Spanish nouns in prepositional
phrases, whereas in English the article is not used

al colegio	$\longrightarrow$	to school
a la escuela	$\longrightarrow$	to school
al mercado	$\longrightarrow$	to market
a la iglesia	$\longrightarrow$	to church
en la iglesia	$\longrightarrow$	in church
en el Congreso	$\longrightarrow$	in Congress

12) with some rivers and mountains

el Vesubio	$\longrightarrow$	Mt. Vesuvius
la Mauna Kea	$\longrightarrow$	Mauna Kea

13) with proper names of persons or animals when
modified
La pequeña María Luisa.
14) given and family names of women may take the
definite article in familiar conversation; sometimes
used also for people in public life, writers, etc.
Ayer vi a la Juana.
I saw Juana yesterday.
La Crawford es una artista famosa.
Joan Crawford is a famous actress.

Object Structures

1. *Lack of correspondence in object patterns:*
Certain Spanish and English indirect object patterns
show an obvious lack of correspondence. This lack of
correspondence is due to:

A. *a complete change of construction between Spanish
and English:*
Example: I like the dress.
In English, ⟨the dress⟩ is the direct object of the
verb; ⟨I⟩ is the subject.
In Spanish, the construction changes completely.
Me gusta el vestido.
⟨El vestido⟩ in Spanish becomes the subject whereas
⟨me⟩ becomes the indirect object.

B. the fact that English requires the use of the preposition resulting in a prepositional phrase as opposed to one word in Spanish (the Spanish indirect object pronoun which expresses the English to, for, from)
Examples:

Él me manda un libro. → He sends a book to me.

Él me compra un
vestido. ──────────→ He buys a dress for me.

or

He buys a dress from me.

Él me lleva los libros. → He took the books for me.

2. *Direct and indirect object pronouns: conjunctive pronouns:*

In English, the position of the object pronouns differs almost completely from the Spanish in that the object pronouns in English will always follow the verb, whereas in Spanish they will precede or follow the verb depending on the particular grammatical structure. The following cases serve to illustrate points of interference and points of similarity between the two languages.

    a) the direct and indirect object pronouns in Spanish precede the verb, whether it be the principal verb in a simple tense or the auxiliary verb in a compound tense. In English, the objects will follow. Example:

Spanish	English
Lo traigo.	I bring it.
Lo he traído.	I brought it.

    b) exceptions to this rule are the infinitive verb forms, the affirmative imperative and the present participle form to which the direct and indirect object pronouns in Spanish follow the verb and are orthographically annexed to it. Here, there is no syntactic difference between English and Spanish except that in Spanish the pronoun is orthographically annexed to the verb whereas in English it is not.

Example:

Spanish	English
Tráigalo.	Bring it.
Espero traerlo.	I hope to bring it.
Estoy leyéndola.	I am reading it.

c) the pronoun in Spanish, however, must precede the negative imperative verb form. In English, the object must follow.
Example:

Spanish	English
No lo traigas.	Do not bring it.

d) if two object pronouns occur together, the indirect always precedes the direct in Spanish. In English, two object pronouns do not occur together but rather the indirect will be preceded by a preposition creating a prepositional phrase. In this case, the direct object in English will precede the prepositional phrase.
Example:

Spanish	English
Dámelo.	Give it to me.
Me lo recuerda.	He reminds me of it.

3. *Position of the reflexive object pronoun:*
Rules a, b, c, and d dealing with the position of the object pronouns are also applicable to the reflexive pronoun.
   a) the reflexive pronoun precedes the verb, whether it be the principal verb in a simple tense or the auxiliary verb in a compound tense. In English, the reflexive pronoun will follow.
      Se lavó.
         He washed himself.
   b) the exceptions to this rule are the following verb

forms: the infinitive, the affirmative imperative, and the present participle, in which the reflexive pronoun in Spanish will follow and be annexed to the verb. Here, there is no syntactic difference between Spanish and English, except that in English the pronoun is not orthographically annexed to the verb, although it does follow it.

Voy a lavarme. ⟶ I am going to wash myself.

Lávate. ⟶ Wash yourself.

Está lavándose. ⟶ He is washing himself.

c) the reflexive pronoun does precede the negative imperative verb form.

No te laves. ⟶ Don't wash yourself.

d) when several object pronouns come together, the reflexive precedes either direct or indirect (see 2d for direct and indirect object pronoun order).

El vestido. Me lo hice.

The dress. I made it for myself.

Verb structures

1. *Use of dependent infinitives with or without prepositions in Spanish and in English:*

In Spanish, the dependent infinitive clause is employed much more frequently than in English, especially when both verbs are governed by the same subject. The corresponding English pattern will often include a subordinate clause.

Siento no poder visitarte mañana.

I am sorry that I cannot visit you tomorrow.

Pensaba ir al teatro esta tarde.

I thought that I would go to the movies this afternoon.

A second lack of correspondence between the two languages exists. Although the two languages will employ function words, there are several possible function words in Spanish ⟨a, para, de, con, en, or ø⟩ as opposed to the one function word in English ⟨to⟩ or ⟨ø⟩. (Few exceptions: count on, know how to, in order to.)

Examples:

acostumbrarse *a* + infinitive = become accustomed
$$to$$

acordarse *de* + infinitive = remember *to*

esperar + infinitive = hope *to*

consentir + infinitive = consent *to*

convidar para (or a) + infinitive = invite *to*

contar con + infinitive = count *on*

2. *Use of infinitive after prepositions in Spanish:*

A lack of correspondence between Spanish and English crops up in the syntactical patterns where Spanish uses the infinitive after certain prepositions. English in the corresponding patterns uses the "-ing" form of the verb.

Examples:

Al salir de casa se puso el abrigo.

Upon leaving the house, he put on his coat.

Para subir al cielo se necesita una escalera grande
y otra chiquita. (folksong)

In order to reach the sky (get to heaven), you need
a big ladder and a little one.

Antes de salir voy a lavar la ropa.

Before going out, I am going to wash the clothes.

Después de comer pienso ir al cine.

After eating, I plan to go to the movies.

Siempre sale *sin* avisarnos.

He always leaves without telling us.

Me ha cansado *de* cocinar.

I am tired of cooking.

3. a) To denote the action without expressed actor, Spanish normally uses the reflexive. To denote the same concept in the same cases, English will normally use the passive or subjects like ONE, THEY, YOU.

— When the reflexive verb is used impersonally to denote the English passive, the verb is written in the third person singular, and a subject is neither expressed nor understood. The reflexive construction is connected to the rest of the sentence by an adverb, a conjunction, or an equivalent word.

No se sabe cómo ganó el dinero.

Se dice que él no sabe nada.

— When an inanimate object is expressed, the impersonal construction is also used in both the third person singular and the third person plural. It is commonly used in notices or announcements.

Se habla inglés.

Se vende tocino de cielo.

— If the subject is an expressed noun or pronoun, the verb agrees with the subject. In this case, the reflexive construction is used personally.

Los regalos de Reyes se enviaron por correo.

Churros y chocolate se sirven para desayuno.

b) The reflexive is used to denote reflexive or reciprocal action. In English, the reflexive is expressed by the reflexive pronoun: ⟨myself⟩, and the reciprocal action is expressed by ⟨each other⟩.

— If the subject is a person capable of performing the stated action, then the construction will be understood as reflexive or reciprocal and not passive.

Los novios se escribían muy a menudo.

The engaged couple often wrote to each other.

La niña se mira en el espejo constantemente.

The girl constantly looks at herself in the mirror.

c) Spanish has two other passive forms which are used very often in speech. The passive of action, often referred to as the true passive, and the passive of state, often referred to as the apparent passive.

The lack of correspondence between the two languages arises because the English patterns can be interpreted as either the passive of state or the passive of action, each of which corresponds to a different construction in Spanish.

1) The passive of action in English corresponds to a construction in Spanish using ⟨ser⟩.

The book was written several years ago.

El libro fue escrito hace unos años.

In connection with the idea of action, English would often use an adverbial phrase.

2) The passive of state in English corresponds to the Spanish construction with ⟨estar⟩.

The book was written.

El libro estaba escrito.

The difficulty for the English speaker lies in determining the difference between the passive of state and passive of action.

One can distinguish between the two in either of two ways:

1) English may add an adverbial phrase of time (example: several months ago—hace unos meses, etc.) indicating action.

El libro fue escrito hace unos años.

or

2) if the construction can be changed to the active voice without changing the original meaning and if the word 'by' ⟨por⟩ + an agent can be added to the sentence.

El libro fue escrito por Cervantes.

The book was written by Cervantes.

Cervantes escribió el libro.

Cervantes wrote the book.

C. Miscellaneous Patterns

1. *Use of ⟨hacer⟩ with:*

a) expressions of time
b) expressions of weather

With both expressions, ⟨hacer⟩ will be conjugated in the third person singular of the desired tense. The object of the verb ⟨hacer⟩ is either a noun expressing an element of weather or an expression of duration of time. In English, comparable constructions use the verb 'to be.'

a) ⟨Hacer⟩ *is used impersonally in Spanish to denote duration of time in the following examples:*

—The tense of ⟨hacer⟩ may be used to indicate the past, present, or future:

Hace cinco días que ... It is five days since

Hará cinco días que ... It will be five days since

Hacía cinco días que ...It was five days since

—When the verb following ⟨hacer⟩ covers the entire duration of time, then the same tense used for the verb ⟨hacer⟩ is also used for the second verb.

Hacía cinco años que vivíamos en Madrid.

Hace cinco días que vivimos en Madrid.

—Contrast between tenses in Spanish and English
is shown in the following examples:

Hace dos años que estoy aquí.

I have been here for two years.

Hace cuatro años que estuve allí.

It is four years since I was there.   or

I was there four years ago.

⟨Ago⟩ is expressed by the verb ⟨hacer⟩ in any
tense. When followed by another verb in the present tense ⟨ago⟩ is *not* used in the corresponding
English pattern.

Hace dos años que estoy aquí.

I have been here for two years.

—If the clause including ⟨hace⟩ is the first clause
in the sentence, ⟨que⟩ will generally be used; if
it is the second clause in the sentence, ⟨que⟩
is *not* used.

Hace cinco días que
llovió.   or   } It rained five days
Llovió hace cinco días.   ago.

Hace cinco días que
llueve.   or   } It has been raining
Llueve hace cinco días.   for five days.

b) *Expressions of weather:*

The verb ⟨hacer⟩ is used in Spanish when speaking of weather or temperature; the corresponding
English patterns use the verb ⟨to be⟩.

The following examples illustrate the contrast:

Hace sol durante el día.

It is sunny during the day.

Suele hacer frío durante el invierno en Madrid.

It is usually cold in (during) the winter in
Madrid.

Hace mucho calor en el verano.

It is very hot in the summer.

Hacía bastante viento mientras estuve en la
calle.

It was quite windy while I was out.

The verb ⟨haber⟩ is also used for expressions of weather when one can see the actual phenomenon. ⟨Hacer⟩, though, is used much more frequently and is gradually taking the place of ⟨haber⟩.

Hay sol allí en el jardín.

There is sun in the garden.

Hay luna en la noche.

There is moonlight at night.

Hay neblina.

It is foggy.   There is fog.

In the following case, ⟨hacer⟩ would not be used:

Hay humedad.   It is humid.

And, in the above case, one would say: Está húmedo.

2. *Position of adverbs:*

Although the position of adverbs is more flexible in Spanish than it is in English, certain general principles can be cited defining the position of the adverb with relation to other words in the sentence. As a general rule, (a) the adverbs will follow the verb especially if the verb has an object, (b) if the adverb is one of time, place, or manner, it may precede the verb resulting in a subject-object inversion, and (c) the adverb may precede an adjective.

a) following the verb:

Él habla bien inglés. – He speaks English well.

b) preceding the verb:

Bien lo hace. (Él). – He does it well.

c) preceding an adjective:

Esta pintura es espantosamente fea.

This painting is terribly ugly.

In sentence c, ⟨espantosamente⟩ also belongs to a class of adverbial modifiers. (e.g., like ⟨muy⟩)

Example: Esa pintura es muy fea.

Esa pintura es sumamente fea.

Esa pintura es horriblemente fea.

3. *Personal* ⟨a⟩:

There are some cases in Spanish which require the use

of ⟨a⟩ before a direct object. Various principles can be cited regarding its usage.

a) before a noun object which is a person, or anything considered as such (e.g., a pet), Spanish will use preposition ⟨a⟩:

Estoy buscando a mis tres gatitos.

¿Has visto a María Luisa?

b) before pronouns replacing nouns which express a person or anything considered as such (e.g., a pet):

He visto a la Sra. Domínguez, a quien mandé los regalos.

Prefiero verla a ella mañana.

Personal ⟨a⟩ is omitted in the following cases:

a) if the noun does not refer to a specific person:

Estoy buscando unos mozos.

b) for euphony:

No he visto Ana María might be heard rather than *No he visto A Ana María.*

c) with some verbs:

tener—Tengo dos hermanos.

4. *Position of adjectives:*

As opposed to English, the descriptive or qualifying adjective or the adjective which distinguishes one noun from others of its class will generally follow the noun in Spanish. Aside from the above general rule, there are certain types of adjectives which will either precede or follow the noun.

The types of noun modifiers or adjectives which PRECEDE the noun in the noun nucleus are as follows:

a) determinative adjectives: articles, possessives, ordinal numbers (except in titles, e.g., Carlos Quinto), cardinal numbers, indefinite adjectives and demonstrative adjectives (except stressed forms, e.g., ese tío mío and demonstratives used for effect, e.g., La niña esa nunca termina de molestar.)

b) for stylistic devices, when an adjective is employed poetically or figuratively:

la hermosa doncella

El curioso parlante*

The adjectives which usually FOLLOW the noun are:

a) those indicating physical, mental, moral qualities such as strength, vigor, size:

Él trabaja en ese rascacielos enorme.

b) those indicating nationality or color:

mi prima chilena

esa casa blanca

c) those modified by adverbs:

Es un hombre completamente loco.

d) those which are markedly longer than the noun they modify:

Es una chica extraordinaria.

e) determinatives will usually precede (see 4a): If they are used for effect they may follow.

La niña esa nunca termina de molestar.

f) Past participles of verbs when used as adjectives follow the noun:

Las lenguas habladas se estudian más que las lenguas muertas.

Two or more adjectives:

When two adjectives modify a noun, their placement before or after nouns is determined according to the above principles.

El muchacho grande y gordo.

In both Spanish and English, the adjective most regularly associated to the noun is placed nearest to the noun it modifies. In Spanish, very often both adjectives will follow. In English, the order is reversed.

La gente rica y elegante. → The elegant and rich people

IV. Vocabulary

A. ⟨Saber—conocer⟩, ⟨por—para⟩ and ⟨ser—estar⟩ are perhaps the most salient examples illustrating the problem caused by two or more Spanish expressions corresponding to one English expression. The principles governing the uses of each of these combinations will be discussed presently.

---

* Obra de don Ramón de Mesonero Romanos

1. Saber and Conocer

The Spanish verbs ⟨saber⟩ and ⟨conocer⟩ both correspond to the English verb ⟨to know⟩. It might be easier for a native speaker of English to distinguish between the two verbs by comparing the grammatical constructions in which they are used rather than the meanings which are attached to the verbs themselves. Nevertheless, both can also be followed by a direct object.

The uses of ⟨saber⟩ and ⟨conocer⟩ as distinguished by their constructions are as follows:

SABER	CONOCER
1) ⟨Saber⟩ may be followed by an infinitive: — ¿Sabes esquiar? Do you know how to ski? Saber in this sense means ⟨to know how to do something⟩.	1) ⟨Conocer⟩ may not be followed by an infinitive.
2) ⟨Saber⟩ may also be followed by a subordinate clause: — Sé que viene a las ocho. I know that he's coming at 8. — Él sabe perfectamente bien donde está el libro. He knows perfectly well where the book is. — No sabemos cuando piensan llegar. We don't know when they plan to arrive.	2) ⟨Conocer⟩ may not be followed by a subordinate clause, except when used to mean recognize (see special uses of conocer.)

⟨Saber⟩ and ⟨conocer⟩, when followed by a direct object, do indicate subtle semantic differences. The following examples and explanations are applicable:

SABER	CONOCER
1) ⟨Saber⟩ indicates knowledge of a factual nature about a person or thing. — Él sabe bien el español.	1) ⟨Conocer⟩ indicates familiarity with persons, things or subject matter. — Él conoce bien el español.

Use of ⟨saber⟩ and ⟨conocer⟩ in the preterite tense: structures and lexical meaning differ.

SABER	CONOCER
1) When used in the preterite, ⟨saber⟩ indicates the idea of learning or finding out something which has occurred. —Lo supe a las ocho. I found it out at 8. —¿Supiste lo que sucedió? Did you find out what happened?	1) ⟨Conocer⟩ in the preterite tense denotes the idea of meeting or becoming acquainted with: —Conocí a su madre. I met her mother.

Special uses of ⟨conocer⟩:

   a) ⟨Conocer⟩ may be followed by an infinitive or a subordinate clause only if the meaning expressed corresponds to recognize, that is, to admit or to confess something.*

     —Ella conoce que se ha equivocado.

        She recognizes (admits) that she is mistaken.

     —Conozco haberla ofendido.

        I recognize that I have offended her.

   b) The impersonal reflexive, ⟨se conoce⟩ may be followed by a subordinate clause.

     —Se conoce que ella es una charlatana.

        It is known that she is a gossip.

   c) ⟨Conocer⟩ may replace ⟨reconocer⟩ when used to indicate recognition of a person or thing.

     —Conozco el vestido verde de María porque se lo puso el domingo pasado.

        I recognize Mary's green dress because she wore it last Sunday.

2. POR—PARA:

The lexical items ⟨por⟩ and ⟨para⟩ serve as another salient example illustrating the problem caused by two or more Spanish expressions corresponding to one English

---

° *Note:* ⟨Reconocer⟩ is much more frequently used with this meaning than ⟨conocer⟩.

expression. The subtle differences in usage tend to confuse the native speaker of English. The following principles define the different uses of the two prepositions:

⟨*Para*⟩ *which is more restricted in meaning, is used to denote:*
    a) destination.
           Se va para Chile.
           He is leaving for Chile.
    b) purpose.
           Estudió mucho para obtener la beca.
           He studied a great deal in order to win the scholarship.
    c) time limitations sometimes expressed by the word ⟨by⟩ in English.
           Lo que no se hace hoy se deja para mañana.
           What isn't done today is often left for tomorrow.
           ¡Qué estés allí para las diez!
           Be there by ten.
    d) comparison usually expressed by the words ⟨for, considering that, compared to⟩.
           Para un niño de diez años, es muy inteligente.
           He is very intelligent for a ten-year-old child.

⟨*Por*⟩ *corresponds to the English* ⟨*for*⟩ *when used to indicate:*
    a) ⟨through, along, around⟩
           Pasó por Portillo (Chile) en su último viaje.
    b) ⟨by⟩ expressing agency, mean, manner, unit of measure
           Lo hizo por las apariencias.
    c) ⟨for⟩ in the sense of ⟨because of, on account of, on behalf of, in exchange for, as⟩
           María haría cualquier cosa por el amor que le tiene. (because of)
           Hazlo por mí. (for my sake)
           Le condenaron a muerte por lo que relató el testigo. (on account of)
           Te doy dos dólares por 120 pesetas (españolas). (in exchange for)

Por loca que sea, todavía es simpática.
As crazy as she is, she still is charming.
d) ⟨by⟩ and ⟨for⟩ in oaths and exclamations
¡Por el amor de Dios!
e) one's personal feeling for or opinion toward someone or something
Se vuelve loco por los caramelos.
f) the place in which or near which an action occurs
Siempre paso por la biblioteca después del
trabajo.
g) the duration of an action
¿Por cuánto tiempo se quedaron acá?

3. USE OF ⟨SER⟩ AND ⟨ESTAR⟩:

The use of ⟨ser⟩ and ⟨estar⟩ with predicate adjectives
is probably one of the most difficult lexical problems in
Spanish due to the different connotations expressed by the
verbs themselves. These are not understood by the native
speaker of English. Although this is the point which causes
real confusion, the other uses not involving the predicate
adjective for ⟨ser⟩ and ⟨estar⟩ will first be discussed.

⟨Ser⟩ *is used in the following cases when followed by:*
a) all predicate nouns, pronouns, or adjectives being
used as nouns
María Luisa es española.
Su padre es médico.
b) a prepositional phrase denoting ownership, origin,
or material from which something is made
El libro es de su cuñado.
Mi familia es de Asturias.
La falda es de lana.
c) an expression of time, especially hours of the day or
dates
Es la una.
Es el primero de abril.
d) an impersonal expression
Es posible.
Es imprescindible.

e) to show location which involves definition (e.g., when location is defined in a subordinate clause). (Actual location is shown by ⟨estar⟩.)

En esa tienda es donde suelo comprar los comestibles.

⟨*Estar*⟩ *is used in the following cases:*

a) to express location or actual position

Estamos en Madrid.

Stanford está en California.

Como castigo, el alumno estuvo arrodillado por dos horas.

b) to express location in time

Estamos a 20 de febrero.

c) as the auxiliary for the formation of the progressive tenses

Estamos estudiando mucho.

d) with the past participle to denote a resultant condition or state

La puerta está abierta.

Uses of ⟨*ser*⟩ *and* ⟨*estar*⟩ *with the predicate adjective:*

The essential difference between the two is as follows:

a) Ser: when the verb ⟨ser⟩ is used with an adjective, the adjective describes a permanent and inherent quality of the subject.

Example: José es guapo. = José siempre es guapo.

Guapo is the inherent and permanent quality belonging to José. In this case, the adjective can be said to function as a noun.

Example: José es guapo. = José es (un hombre) guapo.

b) Estar: When the verb ⟨estar⟩ is used with an adjective, the quality denoted by the adjective is only a temporary characteristic of the person and exists for a short while. It can be considered as a new circumstance in which the person finds himself.

Example: José está guapo. = José isn't particularly good-looking but because he is well groomed today one would say: José está guapo.

In this case, the adjective functions as an adjective, a description of the acquired condition of the person.

SUMMARY:

Ser + adjective → inherent characteristic of a person → adjective functions as a noun.

Estar + adjective → temporary quality of a person existing for a fleeting moment → adjective functions as an adjective.

B. FALSE COGNATES

Words which have the same root and thus are similar in their spelling, pronunciation, and meaning are considered cognates.

False cognates are those which have the same root and are similar in spelling and pronunciation but dissimilar in meaning. These false cognates are a source of difficulty for native speakers of English learning Spanish. The speaker of English will tend to transfer the English meaning to Spanish and, consequently, misuse the Spanish word. Perhaps, the only solution is to learn the appropriate meaning.

Listed below are examples of some of the more common false cognates:

Wrong meaning relationship

true meaning relationship

Spanish Cognate	Corresponding English Meaning	English Cognate	Corresponding Spanish Meaning
alumno	student	alumnus	graduado
conferencia	lecture	conference	conferencia
asistir	attend	assist	ayudar
lecturas	readings	lectures	conferencias
listo (a) (adj)	ready	list	lista (noun)

C. ADJECTIVES: CHANGE OF POSITION RELATED TO CHANGE OF LEXICAL MEANING.

In regular usage, the adjective is placed after the noun and is used for the purpose of distinction. If placed before the noun, the adjective describes an inherent characteristic of the noun itself.

Adjective position	English	Connotation
Las princesas ricas	Rich princesses	Some princesses who are rich
Las ricas princesas	Rich princesses	Princesses, in general, are rich

Some adjectives have different meanings depending on their position. When placed after the noun, they usually assume their original (primary) meaning. The most common of these are:

Adjective	Before	After
Antiguo	old, former	ancient
bueno	good (quality)	good (character)
caro	beloved, dear	expensive
cierto	certain	reliable
diferente	various	different
grande	magnanimous, great	big, large
malo	bad, poor	evil
medio	half	average
mismo	very, same, self (with definite article)	-self (without definite article)
nuevo	another, different	new
pobre	pitiable, unfortunate	poor, needy
propio	own, very	suitable, characteristic, -self
puro	sheer	pure
simple	mere	childlike, simple-minded
único	only, sole	unique
varios	several	miscellaneous

BIBLIOGRAPHY OF WORKS CONSULTED DEALING WITH APPLIED LINGUISTICS IN SPANISH

Bowen, J. Donald and Robert P. Stockwell. *Patterns of Spanish Pronunciation...A Drillbook.* Chicago, 1960.

Bull, William. *Spanish for Teachers, Applied Linguistics.* New York, 1965.

Cárdenas, Daniel. *Introducción a una comparación fonológica del español y del inglés.* Washington, D.C., 1960.

Cárdenas, Daniel. Simón Belasco, ed. *Applied Linguistics, Spanish.* New York, 1961.

Navarro Tomás, Tomás. *Manual de Pronunciación Española.* New York, 1957.

Politzer, Robert L. and Charles N. Staubach. *Teaching Spanish, A Linguistic Orientation.* Revised Edition. New York, 1965.

Stockwell, Robert P. and J. Donald Bowen. *The Sounds of English and Spanish.* Chicago, 1965.

Stockwell, Robert P., J. Donald Bowen and John W. Martin. *The Grammatical Structures of English and Spanish.* Chicago, 1965.

INDEX

Intonation

Bowen and Stockwell:	8-25
Bull:	78-88
Cárdenas:	36-56
Cárdenas (Belasco, ed.):	53-59
Navarro Tomás:	255-273
Politzer and Staubach:	86-95
Stockwell and Bowen:	19-34

MORPHOLOGY

Nouns

Bull:	103-110
Cárdenas (Belasco, ed.):	22-23
Politzer and Staubach:	104-105
Stockwell, Bowen and Martin:	41-47

Noun Markers or Determinatives

Cárdenas (Belasco, ed.):	23-24
Politzer and Staubach:	105-106
Stockwell, Bowen and Martin:	64-73

Pronouns

Subject Pronouns

Bull:	127
Cárdenas (Belasco, ed.):	29-34
Stockwell, Bowen and Martin:	51-52

Direct Object Pronouns: conjunctive

Bull:	128
Stockwell, Bowen and Martin:	51-53

Indirect Object Pronouns: conjunctive

Bull:	128
Stockwell, Bowen and Martin:	51-53

Prepositional Personal Pronouns: disjunctive

Stockwell, Bowen and Martin:	51-288

SYNTAX

A. *Verbs*

Indicative Mood

Present tense:
Bull:	155; 157; 162; 163-165
Politzer and Staubach:	145

Imperfect:
Bull:	155; 161
Politzer and Staubach:	142-144
Stockwell, Bowen and Martin:	135-139

Future:
Bull:	153-163; 177
Stockwell, Bowen and Martin:	144-146; 148-152; 160-165

Preterite:
Bull:	155; 157-159
Politzer and Staubach:	142-144
Stockwell, Bowen and Martin:	135-139

Preterite — Imperfect Contrast:
Bull:	166-170
Cárdenas (Belasco, ed.):	37-40
Politzer and Staubach:	142-144

Present Perfect:
Bull:	153-158; 165-166; 171
Stockwell, Bowen and Martin:	141-143; 148-151

Pluperfect:
Bull:	154; 159; 161; 171
Stockwell, Bowen and Martin:	141-143; 148-151

Future Perfect:
Bull:	155; 160-163
Stockwell, Bowen and Martin:	148-151

Subjunctive Mood

Present:
Bull:	122-123; 125

C. *Object Structures*

1. Subject-object reversal
   Politzer and Staubach: 136
2. Position of object pronouns
   Bull: 254
   Cárdenas (Belasco, ed.):   14-18
   Politzer and Staubach: 137-138
   Stockwell, Bowen and Martin: 189-190
3. Position of the reflexive pronoun
   Bull: ·254
   Cárdenas (Belasco, ed.):   14
   Stockwell, Bowen and Martin: 190

D. *Verb Structures*

1. Use of dependent infinitives
   with or without connecting
   prepositions in Spanish and
   in English:
   Politzer and Staubach: 134-136; 139; 150-
                                                  151
2. Use of infinitive after
   prepositions:
   Politzer and Staubach: 139; 151
3. a. Use of the Spanish reflexive
   to denote action without
   expressed actor:
   Bull: 265-273
   Cárdenas (Belasco, ed.):   8-9
   Stockwell, Bowen and Martin: 235
   b. Use of the Spanish reflexive
   to denote reflexive or
   reciprocal action:
   Bull: 265-273
   Cárdenas (Belasco, ed.)   6-7
   Stockwell, Bowen and Martin: 234
   c. The Spanish passive:
   Bull: 292
   Cárdenas (Belasco, ed.):   6-7
   Stockwell, Bowen and Martin: 233-235

E. *Miscellaneous Patterns*

1. Use of ⟨hacer⟩ with:
   a. expressions of time
   Politzer and Staubach: 142
   b. expressions of weather
   Bull: 15
   Politzer and Staubach: 138
2. Adverbs:
   Bull: 158; 160; 161; 177;
                                         18
   Cárdenas (Belasco, ed.):   18; 21
   Stockwell, Bowen and Martin: 166; 195-205
3. Personal ⟨a⟩:
   Politzer and Staubach: 147
   Stockwell, Bowen and Martin: 27; 35-36; 188-189;
                                         286
4. Position of adjectives:
   Bull: 201-206; 227-228
   Politzer and Staubach: 137
   Stockwell, Bowen and Martin: 87-93; 286; 289

VOCABULARY

A. *Two or more Spanish
   words are the equivalent
   of one English
   expression:*

1. ⟨saber—conocer⟩
   Politzer and Staubach;   160-161
2. ⟨por—para⟩
   Stockwell, Bowen and Martin: 208-212; 229-230;
                                         285
3. ⟨ser—estar⟩
   Bull: 291-295
   Cárdenas (Belasco, ed.):   1-6
   Politzer and Staubach: 136-137
   Stockwell, Bowen and Martin: 167-171; 187-188

B. *False cognates*

Politzer and Staubach: 162-163; 165-168

C. *Adjectives: change of*
   position related to
   lexical meaning

Bull: 227-228
Stockwell, Bowen and Martin: 89

Part II.
Suggested Teaching Behaviors for the Foreign Language Teacher[*]

The behaviors which are enumerated and briefly discussed here represent an attempt to describe the essential features of the performance of the good and experienced language teacher. They are based on the observations and experience of the individuals who have elaborated these behaviors, and they are meant to serve at least three related purposes.

(1) *Research:* The criteria are in a sense a series of hypotheses. They must be regarded as tentative until they are validated by further research. If the criteria are used for evaluation of teaching, not only their validity but above all their reliability must be established.

(2) *Evaluation:* The criteria can quite obviously be used for the purpose of evaluating the performance of a teacher. Although their validity and reliability are, as stated above, subject to further research, they do represent the census of a group of experienced teachers, and they do describe the performance to be evaluated in great detail.

(3) *Training:* The behaviors are, of course, also a training instrument. The beginning teacher can be quite

---

[*]The research and development reported herein was performed pursuant to a contract with the United States Department of Health, Education and Welfare, Office of Education, under the provisions of the Cooperative Research Program.

specifically trained to perform according to the criteria—and can be evaluated in precisely the terms of the criteria which have been used in his training.

The concept of establishing specific behaviors and "performance criteria" for the training of teachers is an essential feature of the *Stanford Teacher Education Program,* where it was evolved under the direction of Professor Dwight Allen. The *Suggested Behaviors for the Foreign Language Teacher* represent, in a sense, the adaptation of the performance criteria concept to a specific subject matter with its very specific problems. The behaviors presented herewith have been revised by the undersigned from the original version.

Stanford, California   Diana E. Bartley
May, 1967   Robert L. Politzer

Sample sheet for
Evaluation of Classroom Performance

Sample sheet for: **Evaluation of Classroom Performance**

Teacher: Jane Smith

Evaluator: Robert L. Politzer

Date: November 6, 1967

Performance	Grade[1]	Comment positive	negative
1. Audio-Lingual Activity	6	(e.g. 1, 4)	6a, 7b
2. Presentation of Basic Material			
3. Teaching of Structure	9	1, 2, 6	
4. Teaching of Pronunciation	7	1	3, 5c
5. Teaching of Sound-Letter Correspondence			2
6. Teaching of Reading			
7. Teaching of Culture			
8. Using Visual Aids			
9. Use of Electronic Equipment			
10. Making Homework Assignment			
11. Testing			

[1]Grade on a scale of 10—0: 10 performance by a very superior teacher
5 average

Comment on all types of performance that you observe—*grade* only those which were a substantial part of the class activity (at least about 10%).

I. MANAGEMENT OF AUDIO-LINGUAL ACTIVITIES

The teacher:
1. Makes sure the class knows the kind of response required (Repetition, rejoinder, questions, answers, etc.).
2. Is the center of attention except in cases in which the nature of the activity dictates otherwise (e.g., chain drills).
3. Maintains a balance of group and individual response.
   - (a) Calls for choral response periodically to insure attention and participation of entire class.
   - (b) Calls on students at random so that all students are obliged to remain alert.
   - (c) Takes advantage of volunteer responses when they will serve to speed up or enliven the activity.
4. Rewards correct response by smile, gesture, or word.
5. Handles incorrect response in a positive manner.
   - (a) Avoids embarrassing the student.
   - (b) Elicits correct response quickly from the group, another student, or supplies it.
   - (c) Offers first student another chance after a reasonable amount of time.
6. Handles undesirable attending behavior properly.
   - (a) Does not stop classroom activity to reprimand or argue.
   - (b) Converts disruptions into learning experiences.
7. Handles student questions properly.
   - (a) Conducts class so that questions are rarely necessary.
   - (b) Insists that questions be asked in the foreign language when possible.
   - (c) Answers only legitimate questions relative to the activity.
   - (d) Includes the entire class when answering questions.

1. Audio-lingual activities consist largely of various types of spoken responses to a variety of stimuli. The efficiency of the audio-lingual activities thus depends, to a large extent, simply on the number of responses which the pupils (in chorus or individually) make during a given period of time. Time consumed by faltering, silence, questions as to the nature of the required response, lengthy explanations of what the pupil is supposed to do, etc. represents time wasted. In order to conduct audio-lingual activities efficiently, the teacher must know how to give, in a minimum of time, perfectly clear explanations and directions as to what is required. Instead of giving a lengthy explanation, the teacher can often demonstrate and model the first few stimulus-response exchanges of a

drill himself. He can also, at the beginning of the course, spend some time explaining carefully and with illustrations the types of drills that will be used in the course and how they will be conducted. Once these explanations are given and understood, he can simply refer to the type without having to go over the whole explanation again. Types of drills and specific activities can become associated with specific names, numbers, or even hand signals so that a very brief signal (verbal and/or visual) identifies for the pupil quite unambiguously just what the nature of the audio-lingual activity is. For example:

Teacher makes a statement and points to the pupil: *Repetition.*

Teacher makes a statement, then a circular motion with his right hand: *Choral repetition.*

The teacher makes a statement, then makes a motion indicating a question mark (or puts a question mark on the board) then makes a circular motion: *Choral response transforming the statement into a question.*

2. The nature of audio-lingual activities requires that the teacher have at any and all times complete control over the class activities. His role is not unlike the one of the conductor of an orchestra who must ensure complete and correct participation. Even when individual responses are called for, the whole class should be responding silently (silent response can be indicated through facial expression). The teacher must thus be the center of attention and the source of all activity. Only on very rare occasions may this role be abandoned, for instance, when the teacher arranges for student responses as reactions to stimuli provided by other students (chain drill, enactment of a dialogue, etc.).

Just as in the case of the orchestra conductor, being the center of the activity may necessitate certain specific physical arrangements. Whenever possible, the class should be arranged in a semicircle with the teacher in central position. If such arrangements are impossible, the teacher can move around the classroom during drill activities in order to retain control over all sections of the class.

3. As stated above, maximum efficiency in the conducting of audio-lingual activities demands that all pupils respond all the time, regardless of whether the response called for is individual or choral. The best way of assuring such pupil participation is to switch back and forth between individual and choral responses and to give the stimulus sentences or cues to the class before indicating what kind of response is called for and who is supposed to make it. Certain pitfalls of conducting audio-lingual activities may be pointed out in connection with this statement. One error consists in relying exclusively or excessively on individual responses. This technique has the disadvantage of not giving the poorer or shyer student the opportunity to learn by responding as part of a group (and by following the lead of the better pupils as he does so). Another error is excessive or exclusive reliance on choral response. The danger here is that choral responses mask individual errors and problems and may, of course, give some pupils the opportunity of withdrawing or slackening. Knowing that they will not be asked to perform individually, they may withdraw from the activity altogether. A third error is indicating the type of response (choral or individual) or the pupil required to give the response *before* the stimulus or cue is given. The result of this procedure may be that those who know that they will not be asked to respond will no longer pay any attention to either the cue or the following response. The same undesirable result may, of course, be achieved by any procedure in which the students are called upon according to a rigid, prearranged order (seating arrangement, alphabetical order, etc.).

As soon as a cue is given or a question is asked, there may be students who will "volunteer" for the response. Volunteers should be called upon often enough not to discourage volunteering altogether. Obviously, in situations in which the pace of the class is slackening, the volunteer can be used to speed up tempo. (The teacher rewards the volunteer not only by asking him to respond but also by asking the entire class to repeat his response. Thus his voluntary response—if correct, of course—serves as a model for the entire group.) At the same time, however, the teacher must be careful not to rely excessively on volunteer responses. Otherwise, he runs at least two risks. First, he gives up, in a sense, his position as leader of the class. The activity fast becomes the monopoly of the few volunteers and the teacher will find it difficult to engage the others in the activity. More dangerous, however, is the risk of complacency. By depending too much upon the response of volunteers, the teacher may delude himself as to the achievement of the class as a whole.

4. In the stimulus-response activity taking place in the classroom, it is essential that correct response by the group or by individuals be rewarded quickly and unambiguously. Such reward may take the form of a smile, gesture or word. What is called for is not so much an indication of personal satisfaction or joy on the part of the teacher, but rather an unambiguous signal that, in fact, the response was correct. If this indication does not follow, then its very absence will become one of the indications that the response was *incorrect*.

5. If incorrect responses occur, they must be handled quickly in a manner which recognizes that they, too, are simply part of the pupils' learning experience. If the incorrect response comes from the group, then the teacher must model the correct one and ask the group to repeat the model. (An incorrect response by the whole group is, of course, an indication that something is quite radically wrong—either the teacher's explanations or his expectations.) If an individual responds incorrectly, the correct response can be quickly supplied by the teacher, another pupil or, preferably, the whole group. The teacher will then give the pupil who had responded incorrectly another chance to make the same or a similar response correctly. Depending on the teacher's judgment of other factors (whether the pupil is naturally eager, shy, hardworking but of low aptitude, etc.) he will adjust the amount of time between the correction supplied by others and the

pupil's second attempt at a correct response. In no case, however, should a pupil be embarrassed by being singled out for reprimand or by being obliged to make several repeated and unsuccessful attempts to respond correctly.

Such attempts to force a correct answer from a single student will not only be embarrassing to the student himself but will also result in the breakdown of the group activity and loss of interest on the part of the rest of the class, since the teacher is obviously engaging in an activity of concern only to himself and one individual. Lack of response on the part of individual pupils should be handled in a manner similar to incorrect response. In other words, the correct response is supplied by others and the pupil gets another chance. (Continued absence of any response or continued incorrect response on the part of individual pupils are matters to be taken up in private conference with these pupils.) There are, however, hardly any cases in which either of these situations justifies the teacher's "dropping" the pupil from any activities by no longer addressing individual questions or cues to him.

6. Obviously, the teacher cannot allow individuals to disrupt the classroom activities by various types of behavior (often designed to accomplish just that purpose). At the same time, however, he cannot let disruptive behavior go unnoticed. The lack of any definite reaction on the part of the teacher will only encourage the pupil to continue disruptive behavior, perhaps in even more disruptive and forceful ways. When disruptive behavior (e.g., pupils talking to each other, paying attention to events outside the classroom, making noise with a pencil, etc.) occurs, the teacher can follow two strategies: (a) He can go on with the classroom activity but take notice of the disruptive behavior by facial expression, gesture, etc. Hopefully, this quick, silent, but unambiguous communication that the behavior has been noticed and reprimanded will stop the pupil from pursuing it further; (b) he can take official notice of the behavior and utilize it for a language learning experience. For example, the reprimand can be made in the foreign language (preferably utilizing a pattern which has just been drilled). If the pupil is talking out of line,

making noise, sleeping, etc., the attention of the class can be drawn to him by asking in the foreign language what he is doing. The answer (supplied by the teacher if necessary) can be incorporated in the pattern drill which is going on at the moment. (All of this can be done in the best of humor so that the offending student is not overly embarrassed.) This second way of handling disruptions is particularly applicable if the latter are not caused by individual students but by events outside the teacher's control (e.g., an announcement made over the loudspeaker, workmen making noise in the hallway, a bee buzzing in the front row, a stray dog wandering into the room, etc.). Converting such disruptions into language-learning experiences which are preferably integrated with the lesson, demonstrates to the pupils that the teacher and his purposes are in absolute control of the situation. Obviously, neither of these two methods of dealing with disruptions or undesirable pupil behavior may work with pupils who are real, genuine "behavior problems." Such cases will probably have to be dealt with in consultation with the principal, vice-principal or guidance counselor. Their handling does not involve the language teacher (in his role as a subject-matter specialist) and will thus not be discussed in this context.

7. To discuss the problem of the handling of student questions in a context of "disruptive behavior" may surprise some. However, we must keep in mind that there are basically three types of questions:

(1) Those which the pupil asks because the teacher *wants him to ask them*—because his curiosity has been deliberately aroused. These questions are, of course, both legitimate and desirable.

(2) Those which are asked because the teacher failed to give an adequate explanation. These questions are legitimate and undesirable.

(3) Those which the pupil asks because he wants to assume control of the class, disrupt the classroom procedure, etc.

Within the context of audio-lingual activities, the last two types of questions loom larger than the first. It may, of course, happen that the teacher may want to "manoeuvre" the pupil into a situation where his curiosity is aroused so that the teacher's explanation comes as a result of the pupil's desire to "find out." The typical situation of a teacher-induced question will arise in the presentation of contrastive patterns. The teacher may model, let us say, sentences of the type: *creo que usted tiene razón* (indicative in the subordinate clause) in contrast to sentences like: *no creo que usted tenga razón* (subjunctive in the subordinate clause) in order to provoke the question: "Why do we use the indicative in one type of clause and not in the other?" However, except in these relatively rare cases in which the teacher wants the question to be asked, questions asked during audio-lingual activity will indicate that the explanations or materials furnished by the teacher have been insufficient. Explanations and instruction must thus be clear and sufficient so that questions of type (2) mentioned above occur only rarely. Questions of type (3) — the illegitimate type — should not be answered at all, but rather handled with a quiet remark that the question is out of place, that the pupil should ask it after class, etc. Ground rules as to which questions are legitimate and which are not should also be clearly established. In general, we endorse the notion that the student should be familiar with the construction of the sentences which he is learning and understand the contribution which each word is making to the meaning of an utterance. If the teacher follows this principle, constructions should be explained as they occur and pupils' questions as to the function of individual words within the construction should be considered as legitimate questions. If, however, the teacher follows the principle, endorsed by some, that at a certain phase of instruction there is no need for the pupil to understand the exact contribution and meaning of each word, then it should be made crystal clear why questions like: "What does this word mean?" "What does this word do?" etc. will *not* be considered legitimate and will not be answered. Ground rules for asking questions should also include some principles as to what kind of questions (if any) may be asked in English. In general, questions should be asked in the foreign language. Insistence on questions in the foreign language will not only reduce the number of "illegitimate" questions but will also keep the class from slipping unnecessarily into English. To this end, the main foreign-language patterns involved in asking questions ("What does this mean?" "I don't understand . . ." etc.) can be taught early in the course.

Finally, the teacher must keep in mind that asking of questions by individual students should never lead to the teacher abdicating control of the class or to the breakdown of the initial teacher-centered unity of the class. A legitimate question worth answering should, almost by definition, be of interest to the class as a whole. Thus, while the question may come from an individual, the teacher's answer must be clearly directed to the whole class. One good way of immediately involving the class in a question-answer exchange is to make a "teacher's question" out of a "pupil's question." Instead of simply answering the question, the teacher readdresses it to the class or to another individual.

II. Presentation of Basic Material

The teacher:
1. Models and drills basic material.
    (a) Exposes students to sufficient number of teacher/tape repetitions.
    (b) Breaks down long utterances into convenient segments.
    (c) Maintains correct pronunciation, intonation and stress pattern.
    (d) Elicits different types of student responses (e.g., individual, group, sub-group. See Management of Student Behavior).
2. Establishes the meaning of new material.
    (a) Uses pictures, realia, and available human resources.
    (b) Uses familiar structure and vocabulary.
    (c) Uses English equivalents when necessary.
3. Provides variety of cues to elicit basic sentence.
    (a) Pictures, realia, or human resources.
    (b) Foreign-language utterances.
    (c) English utterances.
4. Elicits variations of basic sentence.
    (a) Substitution of familiar lexical items.
    (b) Expansion.
    (c) Change of subject and/or tense.

The student speaking a foreign language goes through what might be called a "manufacturing process." He remembers patterns and structures which he has learned and uses these patterns as the "new material" out of which he manufactures the sentences which he wants to form. The goal of language instruction is to make the manufacturing process (which consists of transforming and/or substituting into sentences) as rapid as possible until the student reaches the rapidity of unconscious performance which characterizes the native speaker. But the prerequisite for the manufacturing process itself is the existence of first-class "raw materials." In other words, the student must know as fluently and as accurately as possible an amount of basic material with which the manufacturing process may be performed.

1. The modelling and drilling of basic materials is, therefore, a necessity of language instruction no matter what the specific method employed in the course. Perhaps the most important factor to be kept in mind is simply that the student must have ample opportunity for the acquisition of raw material. The saying of a few sentences by the teacher, a few random repetitions by the students will not incorporate the materials to be learned into the available stock of "raw material." If the "raw materials" are a dialogue, every sentence in the dialogue must be repeated several times. If the raw material is the discussion of a reading selection, then the answer must be modelled and elicited several times until it becomes a part of the automatically available responses on the part of the student.

The modelling of materials is itself a procedure that must be approached with great care. Most well-written textbooks will, of course, avoid the presentation of basic materials which are too complex in structure to be easily learned by the student. But even structurally simple sentences may be too long to be remembered easily by the student. The memory span varies, of course, with individual students, but even with the most gifted student it will be considerably less than with the teacher who is familiar with the language. The teacher must therefore be careful to present for repetition only utterances (or segments of utterances) which the student can handle, but they must then be reassembled so that the student has the opportunity of saying the complete utterance after he has learned the component parts.

The breaking down of longer utterances into small segments poses the problem of maintaining correct pronunciation, intonation and stress throughout the presentation of basic materials. It is difficult to pronounce a segment of an utterance without distortion, yet the teacher must be careful to model the segment with the intonation and stress that will apply when the total utterance is learned. (It is precisely at this step that the tape recorder can be most effective. An utterance can be segmented without distortion and repeated unceasingly on magnetic tape. The tape recorder can provide variety as well as the opportunity for the teacher to move about the room and listen to the students while they are repeating after the taped model.) Other, more obvious, errors to be guarded against are simple mispronunciation, inappropriate intonations (due to constant repetition of the material by the teacher) and overemphasis on elements which the teacher thinks are *grammatically* important.

During the modelling and repeating of basic materials, it is especially important to vary the type of student response. Since the learning taking place is primarily one of "echoing" responses, choral repetition can, of course, be used a great deal. At the same time, it should not be used to the exclusion of other types. Asking for responses from subgroups (e.g., one row only, girls only, one part of the room, etc.) and from individuals not only provides an element of variety, it also gives the teacher the opportunity to check participation and accuracy.

2. In order for the basic materials to be useful in a "communication" manufacturing process, they must mean something to the student. A dialogue or paragraph which has been memorized without comprehension is fairly useless in any further language-speaking experience (even though the student may be perfectly capable of reciting

the entire material upon command). *Unless the student knows what the basic material means, it cannot possibly become the basis for construction and self-expression.* The meaning of the basic material must, therefore, be supplied in the learning process. How best to supply the meaning of basic materials is a debated point in methodology. The advocates of the "direct method" insist that the meaning be supplied through realia, pictures, dramatization or through the foreign language, using, of course, only the vocabulary and structure with which the student is already familiar. The rationale behind the "direct method" approach is that the elimination of English during the process of acquisition of basic material will minimize the interference coming from English and will establish for the student habits which will enable him to associate concepts directly with foreign-language symbols without going through the intermediary of his native language. Some experienced teachers, however, find that rigorous adherence to a direct-method approach may become difficult and uneconomical at times and prefer to establish meaning through giving English equivalents. The recommendation made here is to avoid using English regularly as a means of establishing meaning (to avoid forcing the student into the habit of approaching all of his foreign language via English) but to have recourse to it in those cases in which the direct-method approach turns out to be extremely complicated or unfeasible.

3. In the process of teaching basic material, we can never lose sight of the fact that the acquisition of the material is not the goal in itself. It is "raw material" to be put to work and must be available when needed. One of the prerequisites of availability has been noted already, namely comprehension of meaning. Another factor associated with availability is the number and variety of cues that have been used in the learning of the material. If an utterance has been learned only as the response to a single cue, then it is quite likely that it may never be recalled except in response to that particular cue. If the utterance has been "overlearned" in connection with a response-

linked cue, it may indeed become very difficult to tie the utterance to any *other* cues or stimuli. Sentence 5 of a dialogue, reproduced continuously in response to sentence 4, may become completely unavailable unless sentence 4 is said first. This situation is not unlike that which one experiences quite often if one tries to recall a line of a poem. The entire poem must be recited until one gets to the line one wants to remember. Each line of the poem has been overlearned as a response to the cue of the preceding line. In order to avoid this kind of one-sided "freezing" to a single specific cue, a great variety of cues must be used to elicit the same response. The greater the variety, the greater the probability of recall of the response in a given situation. A basic utterance should, therefore, be associated with (cued by) a picture, an action, a question, a foreign-language equivalent or even an English equivalent. The English equivalent (unless we want to adhere to the "direct method" doctrine) is perhaps the cue most likely to be associated with the utterance in the situation of eventual need. Thus a sentence like *Hace buen tiempo hoy* (It's nice weather today) could be cued by a picture of the sun shining, by a question *¿Qué tiempo hace hoy?*, *¿Qué es lo contrario de "hace mal tiempo"?*, or simply by *It's nice weather today.*

4. Immediately after (or even during) the process of teaching the basic material, there should take place exercises which demonstrate to the student the ways and means of utilizing this basic material for the creation of new and different utterances. Whenever possible, the student should be made aware of the patterns of basic utterances through exercises in which different lexical items are substituted in the basic sentence. After the student has grasped the fact that the basic utterance is not simply a sentence but represents also a *pattern* which can be used to "generate" numerous sentences, variations of the basic pattern itself may be introduced. The basic pattern may be expanded by the addition of new elements or may be slightly modified by such grammatical manipulations as tense changes, changes in number or person of the subject,

etc. To illustrate: a sentence like *Hemos ido al cine* could

(a) become the basis of a substitution exercise in which *al cine* is replaced by *al teatro, a la escuela,* etc.

(b) be used in an expansion exercise in which elements like *ayer, con nuestros amigos,* etc., are added to the basic sentence, perhaps in response to questions like *cuándo, con quién,* etc.

(c) be transformed by the use of different person or tenses in response to questions like: *¿Solía usted ir al cine el año pasado?, ¿Irá usted al cine mañana?, ¿Va su hermana al cine también?*

III. Teaching of Structure

The teacher:

1. Chooses the model sentence carefully so that the pattern being presented is clear.

2. Uses appropriate gestures and/or visual materials to help set the pattern.

3. Models and repeats sufficiently for the class to grasp the pattern and provides for the appropriate amount of student repetition.

4. Explains the mechanics of new drills carefully so that students may know what is expected of them.

5. Employs a variety of cues (e.g., pictures, words, gestures, phrases, realia, classroom environment).

6. Employs an appropriate variety of drills (e.g., repetition, substitution, transformation, expansion, communication).

7. Maintains correct pronunciation, intonation and stress and insists that students do the same.

8. Maintains a well-paced tempo.

One of the most important activities of the language classroom is the teaching of language structures and, along with it, the so-called "pattern practice" exercises. Before discussing in some detail the desirable ways of teaching structure and conducting pattern practice, some of the assumptions underlying those activities must be clarified. Leaving aside more complicated and precise linguistic definitions, we can state that sentences which exemplify or follow the same grammatical construction are all examples of the same *pattern*. Thus the sentence: "The boy knows the answer" follows the same pattern as the sentence: "This child understands our problem" (namely determiner, noun, verb, determiner, noun). No single sentence can be said to be a "pattern." The "pattern" is the grammatical construction which is behind the sentence and which is capable of being behind (of "generating") an infinite amount of sentences. The goal of the teaching of structure and of pattern practice, then, is *not* to teach a large number of sentences, but to teach the pupil the *patterns* which are capable of producing the sentences while at the same time giving practice in the actual process of *using patterns* for sentence production.

In actual practice, the teaching of structure and pattern practice take the form of the student performing certain operations (substitution, transformation) on a sample or model sentence the pattern (grammatical structure) of which he clearly grasps and understands. The first step in the teaching of structure, then, is to provide model sentences the meaning and pattern of which are clearly understood by the pupils.

1. The model sentences should then be chosen in such a way that they really represent the pattern. Preferably, the model sentence should be made up largely of familiar lexical items so that the student is not faced with the problems of learning new vocabulary and a new pattern simultaneously.

2. The meaning of the sentence which serves as the base of the pattern practice must thus be clear to the student. This meaning can be made clear through gestures, visual aids and, if necessary, explanation in English.

3. Lengthy grammatical explanations in English are usually of very little help — though a short explanation clarifying the grammatical principles or structures may at times be helpful. In general, however, it can be said that accurate presentation of the pattern is more efficient and more important than grammatical explanation. Thus a pattern underlying several sentences can be made clear by putting the sentences on the board and using visual diagramming (e.g., lining up vertically those parts of the sentences which represent the same element of the pat-

tern). What is important is to keep in mind that the model sentence or sentences must be mastered (understood and remembered) in order to serve as basis for pattern practice. The initial phase of pattern practice must include a sufficient number of repetitions on the part of the student until mastery of the model is achieved.

4. Pattern drill itself is, as stated above, essentially an exercise in "manufacturing" new sentences from a model and through a model process. Thus the prerequisite of efficient pattern practice is that the student understands clearly just what he is supposed to be doing during the practice session. Lack of understanding on the part of the student will have two undesirable results: (1) he will fumble during the practice process itself (since he will be unable to give the desired response) and lose time in trying to figure out what the response is supposed to be; (2) he will not be able to achieve the real aim of the practice process, namely the use of the sentence-building procedure which is being practiced as a device to form sentences of his own.

5. The goal of pattern practice is then eventual recall of the pattern (and of the "manufacturing process" tied to it) in a situation of future need. We have already stressed that this recall is more likely to occur if the pattern and the pattern practice process are originally linked with a variety of stimuli rather than just one. The teacher must thus try to link the model sentences as well as the variations of the model sentences with a variety of stimuli and cues. Just as the model sentences can be produced upon various cues (questions, pictures, English equivalents, etc., see "Presentation of Basic Materials") so the pattern practice itself can be cued by the same variety of stimuli. Thus a substitution in a basic pattern can be cued by words, gestures, pictures, realia, classroom environment, etc.:

Basic Sentence:	*I like this book very much.*
Word Cues:	*picture, idea, suggestion.*
Realia:	Hold up a picture, book, fountain pen, etc.

Gesture in classroom
environment: Point to yourself (*I*), some
other student (*you*), a pic-
ture of a person (*he*).

6. The recall and use of the pattern are, of course, also
more likely to occur if the pattern is associated with or can
be derived through a variety of processes rather than just
one. Good pattern practice, then, uses a variety of devices.
It must, of course, *start* with the repetition type of exercise
which leads to the retention of the model and of the pattern itself. Then, however, the pattern can be practiced
through substitution in the model sentence. The next step
may involve an exercise in which the pattern is derived
from the transformation of another similar pattern or serves
as the basis for such a transformation. Then the basic
pattern may be expanded into a somewhat larger one.
Since the ultimate goal is the use of the pattern in actual
conversation, the final step in pattern practice should
be the use of the pattern in response to a "conversational" cue which is completely dissimilar to the pattern
itself and in a real "communication situation" in which
the pattern is likely to occur in actual conversational exchange. To illustrate the variety of drill mentioned above:

Repetition: *We like this book.*

We like this book. Etc.

Substitution (by various cues. See 5 above)

idea . . . . . *We like this idea.*

suggestion . . . . . *We like this suggestion.*

picture . . . . . *We like this picture.*

(gesture for *I*) . . . . . *I like this picture.*

Transformations:

Do you like this book? . . . . *I like this book.*

Do you like this picture? . . . . . . *I like this picture.*

or, Does your neighbor like this book? . . . . .

*Yes, he likes this
book.*

Do I like this book? . . . . *Yes, you like this
book.*

or, Do you like this book? . . . . *No, I don't like it.*

Do you like this picture? ...... *No, I don't like it.*
Expansions: *I like this book.*
Very much .... *I like this book very much.*
Not at all .... *I do not like this book at all.*
More than that one ... *I like this book more than that one.*
Communication Drill: (Questions used in *real* situations involving communication)
Do you like your textbook?
Do you like this kind of exercise?
Which subjects do you like?
Which sports do you like best?
Which subjects don't you like?
or, use of completely dissimilar stimulus to which the pupil is instructed to respond with the pattern just learned.
This book is very nice, isn't it?
Football is my favorite sport. What about you?
I love pattern practice. What about you?
Etc.

7. That correct pronunciation, intonation and stress must be maintained throughout a pattern practice exercise is obvious. One of the main temptations for departing from the correct pattern consists in stressing the elements which seem grammatically relevant to the teacher. (This mistake is somewhat similar to the one made when unstressed conjugational endings are stressed because they are grammatically significant: e.g., Spanish or Latin amó, amás, etc. instead of ámo, ámas, etc.) Since the pattern is likely to be remembered with the pronunciation and intonation with which it was acquired, such errors must, of course, be avoided (e.g., if the pattern practice in Spanish consists in varying the object pronouns in *Ese libro me gusta, Ese libro te gusta, Ese libro le gusta*, etc., stressing the unstressed object pronouns would result in an awkward stress or intonation pattern).

8. Throughout any pattern practice, a well-paced tempo must be maintained and responses must be varied (from individual to group). There are at least two reasons for maintaining the well-paced tempo. Slow tempo—faltering on the part of the student—is, of course, an indication that the pattern or the requirements of the exercise are not understood by the pupil (thus his intonation is, by definition, "wrong") and more basic practice and/or explanation is needed. Furthermore, the pattern practice exercise is likely to be more effective the more opportunity for practice it affords. A *slow* exercise will give fewer opportunities for response than a well-paced one and thus be relatively uneconomical. Slow pacing of any activity may, indeed, result in loss of pupil interest and give rise to distractions and distractive behavior.

IV. Teaching of Pronunciation

The teacher;

1. Is at all times a model for correct pronunciation of the foreign language.

2. Provides sufficient opportunity for imitation and repetition.

3. Makes sure of accuracy through frequent eliciting of individual response.

4. Shows awareness of specific pronunciation problems caused by interference from native speech habits and orthography.

    (a) Has the class repeat words containing difficult sounds.

    (b) Uses auditory discrimination drills.

    (c) Has the class repeat words whose spelling is similar in both the native and the foreign language.

5. Is constantly alert to error and makes corrections when appropriate.

    (a) Isolates problems and demonstrates correct sound production.

    (b) Gives *brief* explanation of sound production when appropriate.

    (c) Does *not*, by positive acceptance, reward incorrect utterances.

1. There are special types of language courses (e.g., programmed materials, self-instructional materials) in which the teaching of pronunciation becomes a special activity by

itself, often preceding the learning of other aspects of the language. However, in the usual language course presented by the classroom teacher, the teaching of pronunciation is usually part-and-parcel of other regular classroom activities rather than a special activity pursued in isolation. Thus, the first prerequisite for the adequate teaching of pronunciation is that the teacher is at all times an accurate model of correct pronunciation habits. If he is not, then he has no other choice but to make the pupils aware of his shortcomings and to use tapes and recordings as models for imitation and practice. To present an incorrect model is inexcusable.

2. The learning of correct pronunciation in the classroom is principally a process of repetition of correct models. Some pupils will be able to imitate correctly without great difficulty; others will need many opportunities for listening and repeating before they approach, slowly, a correct imitation of the models which they are hearing. The teacher must keep in mind that in the classroom (as well as in the language laboratory) the pupil is not necessarily a judge of the accuracy of his imitation. These imitations and repetitions must be under the control of the teacher so that they will contribute to the improvement of pronunciation rather than serve as additional practice in *mispronouncing.*

3. The advantage of choral response in pronunciation as well as in other types of practice is, of course, that it gives a larger number of pupils the opportunity to respond more frequently and often encourages the hesitant, shy pupil to form responses. The disadvantage of choral response — especially in pronunciation practice — is that it hides individual error. Thus choral repetition must be constantly varied with eliciting of individual responses. Students who mispronounce must be made aware of their mistake, usually by the teacher asking for another (usually choral) response, then modelling the expression once more himself and finally asking for another imitation by the student who is mispronouncing. The teacher should also be

aware of the simple fact that mispronunciation is often not the result of inability to pronounce correctly but merely the result of sloppiness, lack of attention, etc. In all such cases of mispronunciation, attention paid to the individual by eliciting and quick correction of individual response is especially necessary and effective.

4. The alert and experienced teacher is aware of the specific pronunciation problems which his students are likely to have. Typically, these problems are the following:

(a) The sounds of the foreign language may be completely new (e.g., French *u* in *rue* or Spanish *rr* in perro)

(b) The student may have difficulty in distinguishing between sounds of the foreign language (e.g., Spanish *r/rr* or French *an/on/un*)

(c) The student may substitute English "near equivalents" (e.g., pronounce a diphthongal word — English *say* for Spanish *se* or French *ses*)

(d) The cause of the error may be "orthographic" (e.g., the student may use the sound reflex of English *g* as in English *general* in pronouncing the French *général*, or the English *ti* in English *nation* for French *nation.*)

In all of these cases in which special interference coming from native speech habits or orthography is likely to cause trouble, correct pronunciation may, even if acquired, be lost again through lack of attention or continued practice. Words containing the "difficult" sounds must thus be singled out for practice and repetition in choral as well as individual response. The student must be made aware of those differences in sounds to which he must pay attention in order to hear and pronounce accurately. Those foreign-language phonemes which the student does not distinguish easily and automatically must be briefly and repeatedly contrasted in class in auditory discrimination exercises. (e.g., The teacher can establish: Word 1: *an;* Word 2: *un;* Word 3: *on.* He can then pronounce one word for the student to identify as 1, 2, 3. Or, in Spanish, Word 1: *pero;* Word 2: *perro* are established. The teacher then says:

perro and the students identify by designating 1 or 2.)
The same technique of auditory discrimination drill must
also be applied to foreign sounds and their English substitutes so that the student learns to avoid the substitution
of the English sound. (e.g., Word 1: English *say;* Word 2:
Spanish *se.* The teacher then says: *say* and the students
identify 1 or 2.) Words in which orthographic interference
is likely to occur must also be singled out for special treat-
ment (choral and individual repetition and response) as
they occur. Words which contain the same kind of orthographic interference can be grouped together in pronunciation drills (e.g., *rosa, beso, mesa,* etc. See Performance
Criterion #5). The carrying over of English pronunciation
habits is especially frequent in the so-called cognates
which, in orthography but not in pronunciation, are like
their English counterparts. Such cognates can be contrasted with the English counterparts and correct pronunciation can be modelled and made the subject of several
repetitions.

5. As a general principle, it may be stated that errors in
pronunciation should not go unnoticed. If simple remodel-
ling by the teacher and repetition by the group of individual do not solve the problem, the teacher must then
isolate the pronunciation problem and model the correct
pronunciation several times, very slowly and carefully. If
this does not produce results, the production of the
sounds must be explained briefly and in very precise and
concise terms so that the explanation is a real help to the
student. In connection with the explanation of sound production, the following must be emphasized: in most teaching situations these explanations are remedial measures,
and it is superfluous to give long explanations on sound
production if all (or at least the majority) of the students
can produce the sound by simple imitation. Thus the
description of sound production may not be necessary at
all or may be reserved for small group work (after class or
during laboratory sessions) as remedial work.
Explanations about sound production must be precise,
and the teacher must give clear and understandable direc-

tions which the student can follow easily. The suggestion to produce a sound "more softly" (a vague term) or to "vibrate the vocal cords" (which cannot be done upon command) is fairly meaningless advice. Probably the best way of teaching the production of sound is to make the student *aware* of what he does with his organs in the production of a *familiar* sound and then introduce in precise terms those modifications which will lead from the familiar to the new (e.g., to teach a pupil to produce the fricative [ƀ] as opposed to the stop [b], the teacher can explain that the lips are kept in the same position as for the /b/ sound in English but slightly apart, permitting a continuous passage of air. The teacher can then explain the distributional pattern of the sounds, indicating that the stop sound occurs in initial position or following /m/ or /n/ and that the fricative [ƀ] is found in any other position.

The correcting of pronunciation errors is, of course, subject to limitations (within the classroom situation, at least). The language teacher is, in a sense, often faced with a two-fold dilemma.

(a) Some individuals may persist in pronouncing certain sounds and intonations incorrectly while the rest of the class has acquired acceptable pronunciation. These few individuals cannot be allowed to take up an undue amount of class time.

(b) Pronunciation is, as we have stated before, usually an activity which is incidental to other classroom activities. How, then, is the teacher to handle (in a question/answer exercise or a structure drill) a response which is grammatically correct but which contains the mispronunciation of one or several sounds?

As general guidelines in these two situations, we suggest that the teacher, while not being about to engage in corrective exercises at the moment when the error occurs, should at least not reinforce the error or hold it up as a possible model by giving it positive acceptance and approval. Mispronunciation by the individual who needs special, remedial work after class or during the lab session can be followed by a regretful or disappointed gesture (and perhaps one correct modelling by the teacher). The mispronunciation recurring in a response pattern drill can be handled in such a way that the grammatical correctness of the response is rewarded while the incorrect pronunciation is noted and, by inference, disapproved (e.g., If a student answers the following question properly ¿*Con quién vas a bailar, con Víctor o con Alberto?* and does not distinguish between the fricative [ƀ] and stop [b], the teacher should praise him with a smile reinforcing his correct answer but at the same time, the teacher should indicate the pronunciation error which the student has made).

V. TEACHING OF SOUND-LETTER CORRESPONDENCES

The teacher:

1. Does not introduce spelling and reading until accuracy in pronunciation has been achieved.

2. Controls sound-to-symbol transfer by use of chalkboard, charts, or overhead projector.

3. Isolates spelling of sound to be taught by means of visual devices such as colored chalk, underlining, etc.

4. Provides opportunity for the students to say and hear the sound as the corresponding symbol is being written.

5. Uses dictation in such a way that it supports the establishment of sound-symbol relationships.

6. Gives continued practice in sound-symbol relationship and drills new spellings of the sounds as they appear.

During the first level of language instruction the teaching of sound-letter correspondences is one of the important regular activities of the classroom teacher. Exactly when sound-letter correspondences are to be introduced first (in other words, how long the initial pre-reading and pre-writing period of a language course should be) is still a debated and debatable issue.

1. As a general principle, however, it can be stated that the student at the first level of instruction should not be made to read or write materials which he has not first learned to pronounce accurately. Since orthographic interference is likely to make accurate pronunciation difficult in any case, it seems only logical that good pronunciation be established before this new interference factor is intro-

duced. The establishment of sound-symbol relation is thus primarily the process of tying symbols to an already established accurate pronunciation. In trying to establish accurate pronunciation and sound-symbol relation at the same time the teacher is forcing the student to learn two unknowns simultaneously. In addition, the possibility of orthographic interference with pronunciation is maximized. Accurate pronunciation before spelling and reading can, of course, be applied to fairly large amounts of material (e.g., the course is begun with a prolonged pre-reading period) or to quite small amounts of material (e.g., audio-lingual practice of a drill precedes writing practice within the same class session).

2. Since the establishing of sound-symbol relations involves associating sounds with visual counterparts, all sorts of visual aids can be employed. Thus the teacher can use the chalkboard, slowly writing phrases as he (and the class) pronounce them out loud. He can use charts which can be read out loud — charts which summarize with examples different ways of spelling the same sound, and which can be part of the permanent classroom display. The overhead projector can be used to project charts or reading selections which are read in chorus or by individuals while the teacher traces the visual counterparts of the sounds that are being produced.

3. In order to make spelling patterns stand out and cause different spellings of the same sounds to become associated with each other in the minds of the students, various techniques can be used quite effectively (e.g., colored chalk, various types of underlining, etc.).

4. During spelling and writing activities it is, of course, particularly important to make sure that spelling and pronouncing really accompany each other. The silent copying of materials will not necessarily contribute to the establishment of a sound-symbol relationship concept. It may, in fact, lead to orthographic interference resulting in mispronunciation, the very pitfall which the delayed introduction of reading and writing is supposed to avoid. Therefore, especially in the initial stages of writing, the teacher

must be sure that writing and simultaneous pronouncing is a classroom (or laboratory) activity *under his control* so that spelling is not accompanied by silence or mispronunciation.

5. Dictation is an excellent exercise to establish sound-symbol relation. However, care must be taken that dictation is indeed the tying of symbols to familiar *sounds* and structures. Thus, dictation exercises which serve the purpose of establishing or reinforcing sound-symbol relations cannot contain unfamiliar items, nor can they be composed of sentences or conversations which are already completely familiar to the pupil, so familiar that he can write them without paying attention to the corresponding sounds. Sentences, paragraphs, etc., which represent new combinations of familiar words and structure and which the pupil repeats out loud before (or during) the writing activity are particularly suitable for the establishment of sound-symbol relations.

6. New spellings of the same sound must be drilled as they appear, and then correlated and brought together with the already familiar spellings, (e.g., jefe, general).

VI. Teaching of Reading

The teacher:

1. Limits reading material, in initial phases, to items learned audio-lingually and avoids, as much as possible, introduction of new vocabulary and structure.

2. Establishes sound-letter correspondences from written materials by means of reading drills (e.g., minimal pairs, words with similar orthographic features).

3. Uses different techniques to assure actual *reading*, rather than recitation from memory, of material learned audio-lingually (e.g., recombination narratives, dialogue adaptations).

4. Uses visual aids and dramatization, where possible, to aid comprehension of reading materials.

5. Utilizes reading materials as a basis for audio-lingual activities by means of detailed questions on *small segments* of these materials.

6. Uses pre-reading helps (e.g., vocabulary, structure annotation).

7. Checks on homework by specific questions, previously prepared.

8. Avoids unguided "reading out loud" (models, if necessary).

Much of what we said about the establishing of sound-letter correspondence (in the initial phases of the teaching of writing) applies of course also to the initial phase of the teaching of reading. Probably the most important aspect of the initial phase of the teaching of reading is simply that it should consist primarily of a process of tying orthographic representation to audio-lingually familiar material. Thus the pupil should not learn "how to pronounce letters" (or words, sentences on written page) but should learn which written symbols correspond to sounds, words, and utterances which he can already pronounce correctly. Again we want to stress that this recommendation does not necessarily imply a prolonged pre-reading period. It can be applied to the sequence of presentation of materials within one single class session.

1. Tying orthographic representation to audio-lingually learned material means, of course, that the initial phases of reading instruction should not be used to introduce new vocabulary or structure — or that any such new vocabulary should at least occur only rarely, dispersed in already familiar material. If the textbook used in a course does indeed make a practice of using reading for the introduction of basic material, then the teacher can present such readings first audio-lingually (e.g., reading and repetition by sentence or paragraphs — preferably with books closed).

2. While the introductory phase of reading must deal with familiar material, the first goal of reading instruction is the establishment of sound-symbol correspondences which will eventually enable the student to use the visual image of the word to reinforce his "acoustic memory" and which will also enable him to produce the correct pronunciation of unfamiliar words and phrases from the written or printed page. To achieve these particular goals reading drills can be used which are similar to the ones described under the heading of sound-symbol correspondence and which go hand in hand with those drills. Again color, underlining, etc. can be used to call attention to the important orthographic features which are being learned. In

order to make the student conscious of sound-symbol correspondences, it is also possible—at a somewhat later stage of reading instruction—to go through exercises asking the student how many sounds there are in a given word (or short utterance)—how often a given sound occurs in a specific utterance (e.g., write the word, *silla*, write how many sounds there are in the word: answer *silla*, 4; or write, *Roberto va en el ferrocarril;* how often does the sound /r̄/ occur in that particular sentence: answer 3; Roberto, fe*rr*oca*rr*il).

3. Since the initial phase of reading instruction consists of tying symbols to familiar material, there is of course the danger that the pupil may reproduce the familiar material from memory without going through any kind of process associating sounds with symbols (just as in the initial stage of writing the student may reproduce written symbols from memory without associating them with sounds). There are several ways in which the danger may be counteracted. First of all, the teacher can, during reading practice in class, watch carefully the reaction of the pupil and use slides, overhead projector, etc. to introduce and pace the readings in such a way that they do not become quick, audio-lingual recitations. Material already learned audio-lingually can be used in different sequences (e.g., instead of reading the lines of a dialogue in the way in which they follow each other, they can be read in different order). Perhaps the best way of assuring actual reading is to recombine the already familiar structure and vocabulary into new materials and to use reading material which presents the already familiar in such a way that it cannot be reproduced without an intervening reading act.

4. As soon as the reading instruction and activity go beyond the stage of simply establishing sound-symbol relations, the teacher must keep in mind that reading activities in the classroom must be part of the total program of learning to communicate in a foreign language. In no case should reading a foreign language be confused with translating from the foreign language into English. Trans-

lation from the foreign language should thus be either not used at all or only very sparingly as an occasional device to assure that the student understands the meaning of what is being read. During the first classroom presentation of readings, however, the teacher should as much as possible make sure that understanding does not come from the continuous presentation of English equivalents, but from context, pictures, or other visual aids supplied either by the text materials or by the teacher, dramatizations, quick explanations in the foreign language. The explanation in English and especially translations into English should be a last resort—chosen for the sake of economy rather than a first choice.

5. One of the best ways of providing for (and checking on) comprehension of reading materials is to make the reading the basis of audio-lingual activity. This interweaving of reading with audio-lingual activity is done best in such a way that very small segments of material (e.g., a sentence or a short paragraph) are read and then made the immediate object of detailed and analytic questions. Such a procedure not only checks upon real comprehension, but it also brings about the immediate conversion of the readings into the audio-lingual domain while the constructions and vocabulary are still fresh in the mind of the student.

6. In the first stages of language instruction (level 1, possibly 2) the main flow of material is always from an initial audio-lingual contact to the realm of reading and writing. On the advanced levels (3, 4) the direction of the flow can be reversed. In other words, materials are assigned first for reading at home, then for subsequent class discussion. The amount of time and importance devoted to reading increase. It is particularly important at the more advanced levels that the teacher must take care not to suddenly adopt procedures which in fact force the pupil into bad reading habits, or painful translation from the foreign language to English. Audio-lingual preparation (e.g., reading out loud in class, choral repetition, etc.) of texts may have to be continued into the more advanced

levels of instruction. Special care must be taken not to use homework assignment materials in which the amount of new vocabulary introduced per line is so large that it is in fact impossible for the pupil to read the materials in the foreign language. If too much new vocabulary is introduced at once, the pupil is forced to look up the words before reading the material; in other words he will probably write the English equivalent in the book, then attempt to make out the foreign language structures and meanings on the basis of the vocabulary equivalents. This is reverse of the procedure implied in reading the foreign language. The pupil should understand what he is reading as the basis of the already familiar structures and vocabulary, guess the new vocabulary from the structural and situational context, and then confirm, if necessary, his guesses by looking up the unfamiliar words in the dictionary. If texts are introduced in which there is a large amount of unfamiliar vocabulary and structure, then the textbook, or the teacher, must make sure that most of the vocabulary and structure are anticipated and presented to the pupil before he is asked to read the text (e.g., the new vocabulary can be explained in the foreign language, illustrated by a sample sentence similar to the one in which it occurs in the reading, or sample sentences illustrating the complicated structures found in the text can be put on the board and briefly explained).

7. On the more advanced stages the discussion of materials read at home becomes a fairly frequent and typical classroom activity. The teacher must then be careful to prepare for this discussion. He can focus the student's homework on special sections of the reading or announce the questions to be discussed in class, ahead of time. He can carefully prepare questions about the homework so that the classroom discussion follows the plan mapped out by the teacher. Those special portions of the reading assignment which contain key passages, constructions of special difficulty, etc. must be singled out for questions. While the teacher should, of course, answer all legitimate questions, and while it may at times be indeed desirable to lead the

student to ask questions, the discussion of a reading assignment should never become a question-and-answer period in which the students do in fact ask the questions and in which the teacher has abdicated this role of being responsible for the conduct of the class.

8. Even at more advanced levels, reading "out loud" of extended passages by individual students is an activity which must be handled with some care: If the student can indeed read and pronounce well, he does not need the practice. If he does need it, he should not become a model for the rest of the class. Thus the teacher must remain the primary model for accurate pronunciation. Reading out loud on the part of the student must be primarily imitation of the teacher and must be followed by reading on the part of the teacher who then becomes the model for further choral and/or individual repetitions.

VII. Teaching of Culture

The teacher:

1. Relates cultural material as closely as possible to Foreign Language instruction.
   (a) Is alert to the possibilities for cultural exposition inherent in the basic material.
   (b) Integrates, where possible, outside cultural experiences and materials with the basic material.
   (c) Does not go beyond the linguistic level of the class in his choice of cultural materials (songs, poems, history, art, etc.).

2. Takes advantage of all available real products of the country when introducing culture on all levels (records, newspapers, magazines, realia, etc.).

3. Uses culture positively and not as a stop-gap or time-filler.
   (a) Does not consistently reserve the last minutes of the class or Friday periods for the presentation of culture.
   (b) Enlivens the period by judicious choice of the moment to introduce cultural material.
   (c) Uses the cultural material to re-establish the working set of the class.

There are at least two definitions of culture which seem to have current validity. One takes the view that culture represents the outstanding achievement (artistic, literary, musical, etc.) of a particular people. This is the point of view typically represented by college departments of language and literature. The other view is that culture represents the "learned and shared behavior" of the individuals of a given community and includes all institutions or products of human activity, at least inasmuch as they are the outcome of such learned and shared behavior. The latter view is the one which is at the basis of the work of the anthropologist or perhaps, more generally speaking, of the social scientist. A great deal of confusion can arise if the two conflicting definitions are not carefully separated. For the language teacher both definitions of culture, the artistic-literary view (Culture with a capital C, as it is sometimes called) and the anthropological view (culture with a small c) are important and relevent. Besides, both views represent at times only complementary ways of looking at the same thing: a great work of art (e.g., a novel) can be viewed as belonging to "Capital C" as well as "small c" culture – about which it may also contain a great deal of important information.

1. Of course, many of the outstanding products of Culture use the medium of language, and all language is part of culture (it is the "learned and shared behavior" *par excellence!*). Small-c culture is part-and-parcel of foreign language instruction. The foreign language operates, normally at least, in the foreign culture. Its vocabulary and structure are used to refer to objects, institutions, customs, etc. which exist in that foreign culture. To teach the foreign language as if it referred primarily to the familiar cultural environment of the native English of the pupil is a falsification which at the same time also removes much of the motivation for language study and makes it appear trivial: why learn a foreign language if it seems to be only an alternate way to refer to the already familiar cultural environment? In order to make the study of language relevant, the pupil must be constantly reminded that the foreign language is, indeed, not an alternate way to refer to the familiar, but that it is a new and different means of communication used in a different cultural environment to which it is the primary and most direct way of access.

The presentation of foreign culture must therefore be tied to the teaching of the foreign language as closely and intimately as possible. Even in the most elementary stages, the point that the foreign language operates in a different reality can be made briefly whenever the opportunity arises (e.g., windows, bathrooms, loaves of bread, etc. in France do not resemble their American counterparts). The teacher must thus be able to utilize every possibility inherent in the basic materials to alert the student briefly to the fact that, behind the language which he is learning, there is a culture different from his own.

Many teachers will, of course, supplement the basic materials used in the language course by other materials specifically designed to make the student aware of the foreign culture. Such cultural additions (small-c as well as capital-C) can be very valuable. Extreme care must be taken, however, that the presentation of such materials helps, rather than hinders, the process of learning the language. If the materials are not integrated with the course, then the presentation will be perceived as an activity separate from, or artificially superimposed upon language instruction. The material will neither motivate nor reinforce the foreign language learning experience.

Two errors must be especially guarded against: one is the excessive amount of presentation of cultural material in English; the other is the introduction of language materials (songs, poems, stories) which are linguistically far beyond the level of the class. In order to point up the intimate connection of language and culture and in order to act as a motivating force, the materials must have a connection with the foreign-language experience — must preferably be in the foreign language and at the same time within the possible linguistic reach of the pupil. In other words, let us say, a movie on Southern France narrated in English more or less arbitrarily imposed on the instructional process has little or no value. The same movie, shown following the reading in French of a short story taking place in Southern France will have more value, since it gives the pupil a look at the cultural environment of the preceding linguistic experience. The same movie in French, but incomprehensible to the pupil, will mean very little. However, if this film is introduced at a time when it is linguistically accessible to the pupil, when perhaps its script can be "prepared" in class and made the object of discussion and exercises, this same movie will be a valuable cultural adjunct intimately tied to the pupil's language experience.

2. Perhaps the best way of making the culture behind the language real to the pupil is the introduction of realia representing the culture. But realia must also be chosen in such a way that they are, whenever possible, connected with the regular instructional program and within the reach of the pupil. Realia representing the foreign country do not only include objects (food, articles of clothing, etc.) but, especially on the more advanced levels, they may consist of real specimens of the language (newspapers, magazines, commercial phonograph records, etc.) and last, but not least, native speakers used as resource persons. Again it should be stressed that the use of foreign language realia must, whenever possible, be prepared and be made part of the total instructional program. The songs on a record can be explained and written on the board and may, indeed, be chosen to illustrate a language pattern which has just been learned.

3. Since the presentation of cultural materials is an important and necessary part of language instruction, it should not consistently be used as a stop-gap or time-filler during periods when the attention of the class slackens. The teacher who consistently assigns the last few minutes of the class session or part of the Friday session to the presentation of culture because "that is all that could be accomplished during these periods anyway" not only admits defeat in his effort to retain and maintain the interest of the class, he also, by implication, assigns to cultural material an inferior status. Loss of pupil interest during certain periods of instruction should be counteracted by

various means and not assumed as inevitable and frozen into the structure of the course.

Thus the teacher, instead of assigning culture presentation to the periods of slackening in attention, could try to keep these periods from occurring by using presentation of cultural materials for a change of pace or to arouse interest before the drop in attention occurs.

There is, of course, a danger inherent in the introduction of cultural material for the purpose of preventing a drop in pupil interest. If the material is not connected with the lesson as such, it may perhaps attract attention and interest *per se*, but it will constitute a break in the continuity of the lesson and, after the cultural diversion, return to the normal progress of the lesson as such may become difficult or impossible. The cultural digression should thus be chosen in such a way that it has some connection with the basic material being presented and that it also affords the possibility of a smooth return to the language-learning activity. For example, a pattern used in pattern practice and connected with "asking for" objects may be used for a digression on French "specialized stores" versus the American supermarket and the increasing number of American-type supermarkets in France, etc. Following this, an exercise in which students ask for different items in a bakery, grocery store, etc. can be used for the return from the cultural digression to the language-practice activity.

VIII. USING VISUAL AIDS

The teacher:

1. Uses visual aids to illustrate and clarify structure and spelling (e.g., charts, chalkboard, flash cards, pictures, overhead projector).

   (a) In correction and confirmation of homework.
   (b) In teaching sound-letter correspondences.
   (c) In introducing new words in the reading/writing stage.
   (d) In teaching grammatical concepts (e.g., verb endings, agreement, etc.).

2. Uses visual aids as cues to support language activity (e.g., realia, pictures, drawings, etc.).

   (a) In supplying meaning.
   (b) In stimulating conversation.
   (c) In cued response.

    3. Uses visual aids actively or on the bulletin board to relate
culture with classroom activities.
      (a) Uses posters, magazine ads, newspapers, etc. which
are products of the foreign language culture.
      (b) Uses visual aids which are related to and illustrate as
closely as possible the cultural topic being discussed.
    4. Uses visual aids of high quality and appropriateness for
maximum effectiveness in teaching.
      (a) Aids should be visible to, and identifiable by, the
entire class.
      (b) Aids used to convey meaning should be completely
unambiguous.
      (c) Aids should not be unduly distractive.

1. Visual aids can be used, first of all, in direct support
of the teaching of language as soon as writing is introduced
in the course. In a sense, writing itself and the use of the
blackboard to clarify words or constructions in writing is
the most obvious visual aid of the language instructor.
When writing has been introduced, and especially during
the process of introducing writing and sound-symbol correspondence, this particular visual aid should be used as
often as possible. While in the first-level language instruction it is generally desirable to have audio-lingual contact
and audio-lingual practice precede the introduction of
written equivalents, the teacher should never neglect the
use of writing and thus "throw away" the powerful help
which many pupils (especially "visually-minded" pupils)
receive from being able to associate the spoken word with
a written, visible counterpart.

The blackboard (or other ways of showing the written
equivalents of language) should thus be used in a variety
of activities; e.g., the correction of homework (see X, 4b),
the teaching of sound-letter correspondences (see V, 2),
the introduction of new words as soon as their correct
pronunciation has been established.

Various devices can be employed to make the use of
writing particularly effective. In the establishment of
sound-symbol correspondences, the same underlining or
color can be used for symbols corresponding to the same
sounds. The teacher can reinforce grammatical concepts
by writing structurally identical or similar sentences in
such a way that these identical elements are lined up in

vertical columns. Structurally equivalent endings can be written in the same color or underlined in the same fashion. Agreements between words can be made clear by identical colors or underlinings or arrows connecting the endings which must be in agreement.

2. A very different type of visual aid is represented by the pictures, drawings, or realia which can be used in support of language activity. One very popular way of using such aids is for the purpose of supplying the meaning of the utterance or words that are being introduced. The so-called "direct method" consists of using visual aids almost exclusively for this particular purpose; but even the teacher who does not strictly adhere to a "direct method" approach will find that talking about visually present realia (including pictures, actions, etc.) is an effective way of providing a frame of reference for the introduction of new material and to reinforce language learning, since activity that is associated with a picture or object will probably be remembered better than activity which is introduced without visual tie-in.

Aside from providing meaning, visual aids can thus also be used to provide a frame of reference to give the class and the teacher something concrete to talk about. A picture can serve as a useful stimulus to conversation. The description of the picture itself can in turn be used for eliciting responses from the student.

Pictures can also, in a rather specific way, be used as cues in different types of pattern practice. Thus, as soon as the pupil has learned to associate a particular vocabulary item with a picture, the latter, rather than the word itself, can be used as stimulus in a substitution type of exercise (e.g., the basic sentence may be *The teacher is in the classroom.* The teacher holds up the picture associated with the principal. Student's response: *The principal is in the classroom).* Another possibility consists in having the pupil associate a specific basic utterance with a picture and then using the picture to cue the utterance or, perhaps, transformations of the utterance (e.g., a basic sentence like: *The teacher is looking at the homework* is associated with a picture. The picture itself can now be used to cue this sentence. The pupil can then be taught to transform the basic sentence upon receiving supplementary cues. The picture, in conjunction with the cue: "yesterday" can be used to cue the response: *Yesterday the teacher was looking at the homework*, etc.).

3. Generally, the visual aids which can be used to illustrate the culture of which the foreign language is a part (posters, bulletin board displays, realia, etc.) are not quite so intimately related to the language-learning activity, yet their effectiveness will largely depend on making their relation to language and language learning as close and intimate as possible. The main purpose of "cultural realia" is to make the foreign culture real and to remind the pupil that the language is a real activity carried on by real people—not merely a classroom exercise. Posters, magazines, real products of the foreign culture should thus be used as visual aids as much as possible and, whenever possible, in *close relation to classroom activity*. The pictures or drawings used to provide meaning can be made in such a way as to convey the idea that they are representing individuals or artifacts of the foreign culture. The realia brought to class to aid in teaching, let us say, the different colors, the definite article, etc., can be products of the foreign culture. The picture on the bulletin board showing *Notre Dame de Paris* or *El Escorial* are indeed the subject (or at least related to the subject) of the current lesson.

4. The visual aids themselves should be of high quality and effectiveness. There are a few fairly obvious guidelines:

A visual aid must, by definition, be visible and easily perceived by the entire class (not just the front row). Thus, the teacher must guard against small, illegible writing, confusing blackboard presentation (e.g., leaving distracting items on the board) small pictures or realia, etc.

If the visual aid is used to supply meaning, then it must be completely unambiguous. This question of ambiguity is less of a problem if the teacher does not adhere strictly to the "direct method," provides meanings in English, or uses the picture merely to cue an agreed-upon word or construction.

A final point to be considered is that visual aids should always be used in support of language activity but should not be allowed to become dominant over it. Thus the detail, content, even aesthetic quality of a visual aid must be carefully considered in relation to the activity for which it is used. A very beautiful painting may be a wonderful example of cultural achievement—a beautiful slide picture may give a very good view of certain aspects of a foreign culture—and both may be used effectively as the basis of description to provoke conversation, but their very richness and beauty may turn out to contain too many distractions to make them useful vehicles for cuing in pattern practice or for serving as a frame of reference in the introduction of a grammatical concept.

IX. USE OF ELECTRONIC EQUIPMENT (LANGUAGE LABORATORY)

The teacher:

1. Makes sure that the pupils are thoroughly familiar with the content of the material before it is drilled in the lab.

2. Makes sure that the class understands the mechanics of the drills.

3. Monitors the work in progress.

    (a) Makes sure that all pupils are participating actively.

    (b) Provides for positive reinforcement in such a manner as not to interfere with the drill.

    (c) Is alert to pupil error and makes provision for individual correction where possible.

    (d) Stops the drill when it becomes obvious that the class is not benefiting from it.

4. Adjusts the frequency and duration of drills.

    (a) Uses the equipment only when appropriate.

    (b) Uses the equipment only as long as necessary.

5. Adjusts to the exigencies of scheduling by using profitably any time in excess of that which is needed for overlearning, (e.g., songs, comprehension exercises, short stories, riddles, filmstrips, pictures).

6. Follows up the laboratory drills with appropriate classroom activities, (e.g., variations in structure and/or vocabulary, recombination of structural items, testing of the specific structures drilled).

Before discussing the behavior of the teacher in connection with language-laboratory activities, a few points concerning laboratories and their use must be elucidated. Laboratory work will, of course, vary according to the type of installation that is used, the type of scheduling and the general framework within which the laboratory is utilized. Regarding types of installation, we must distinguish:

(1) the laboratory which is a mere listening facility. (Level One)

(2) the laboratory which allows for listening to recorded material and also to the student's own voice through activated earphones. (Level Two)

(3) the laboratory which allows not only for listening but also for recording of responses and which makes it possible (because of a tape deck at each student position) to play back the student's recorded response. (Level Three)

In the use of the laboratory, the following situations must be clearly distinguished:

(1) The laboratory is used to allow maximum flexibility in instruction in the sense that each pupil (or at least group of pupils) can progress at his own optimal speed of learning. In this type of utilization, the laboratory is the place where the core of the learning experience takes place. Utilization of the laboratory for this type of learning requires the use of self-instructional (programmed) or at least partly self-instructional materials.

(2) The laboratory facilities are available to the student according to his needs or interest (the "library-type utilization"). In this type of utilization, the language course itself progresses at the same speed for all students, but the supplementary practice afforded by the laboratory can vary from student to student.

(3) The laboratory is a fixed part of regularly scheduled instruction (nonflexible use). During certain parts of the class hour or during other regularly scheduled periods, all students are exposed to

identical time blocks of exposure to laboratory materials.

While the flexible use of the laboratory (Situations 1 and 2 above) is probably the most interesting and promising, the nonflexible use (Situation 3) is, at present, the most typical, at least on the high-school level. In this nonflexible use, the laboratory is not (as is the case in Situation 1 above) the place where initial learning of materials takes place. It is rather the place for practice and "overlearning" of material with which the student already has some familiarity. The main advantages of the use of the language laboratory in the nonflexible situation consist in the possibility of providing a variety of correct models, of giving the student the opportunity to make a much larger number of individual responses than he could make during a comparable classroom period and, last but not least, of giving the teacher some relief from continuous and strenuous audio-lingual drill activities. Our discussion of teaching activities in connection with the laboratory will, then, be primarily concerned with Situation number 3, the relatively nonflexible utilization.

Perhaps the most important overall consideration in the use of the laboratory is that the laboratory work must be an integral part of the total instruction, not a separate entity, and that therefore, the transition from classroom activities to laboratory activities (and back to classroom activities) must be natural, smooth and quick. If the laboratory work becomes, in fact, an interruption of the normal flow of instruction rather than a helpful continuation, it becomes uneconomical and self-defeating.

1. The laboratory, usually by the very nature of its physical layout, is not the ideal place in which to explain or to introduce new material. Especially in the initial stages of instruction, it is necessary that the teacher watch each individual student's intonation and pronunciation as new material is introduced. In the laboratory, this task of keeping track of the entire group is extremely difficult. Even the most accurate "hi-fi" equipment (and most laboratories will *not* qualify for that description) will allow some dis-

tortion in the pronunciation which may be imitated by the student. Presentation of basic material in class rather than in the laboratory not only gives the teacher the opportunity to observe and correct immediately, it also gives the student the help which comes from watching the facial expressions (lip movements, etc.) which accompany pronunciation. The laboratory work should thus, normally at least, not represent the student's first exposure to basic materials. This does not, of course, exclude the possibility that drills, exercises which represent variations of basic materials, or "overlearning" of basic materials be made part of the laboratory sessions.

2. If the laboratory work consists of exercises of the structure-drill type, then it is essential that the students know what the exact nature of the drill is, either by means of brief instructions before the beginning of the lab session or via instruction on the tape or both. Instructions for laboratory work need to be even more concise and unambiguous than instructions for classroom activity. In classroom activities, a puzzled look on the faces of some students, a raised hand, a faltering response will provide immediate feedback as to the lack of clarity of the instructions, and the teacher can quickly retrace his steps and restate the explanations. In laboratory activities, the lack of unambiguous clear description can usually not be remedied very easily. It often takes longer to find out that instructions have not been understood, and so the teacher may find it more difficult to retrace his steps in order to clarify the explanation. Then, too, the teacher may not even be on hand when the "breakdown in communication" takes its effect, in which case, of course, the student may go through the whole session without knowing what he is doing.

3. We have stated before that the main advantage (at least of the nonflexible laboratory) consists in maximizing the number of responses made by the individual student. In connection with this statement, a few simple facts must

be kept in mind. During the lab period the teacher must make sure that:

    (a) student responses do in fact occur

    (b) responses are made attentively

    (c) the essential practice of rewarding correct responses and correcting wrong ones is maintained at all times.

Of course, tying in the language laboratory work very closely with classroom instruction will go far toward accomplishing at least some of the above-mentioned goals. However, monitoring in the lab is usually a necessity. The teacher can monitor the work by listening from a central listening console or (at times even more effectively) by simply walking up and down and observing the performance of the students. Those who are responding attentively and correctly can be rewarded (by an encouraging smile or by a quick verbal reward via the console), and students who are not responding or who are responding incorrectly can be singled out for individual encouragement and/or correction. Much of the laboratory work included in current textbooks is based on the assumptions that the student can indeed judge accurately whether or not he has made a correct response, that he can make this judgment on the basis of comparing his response with the one provided on the tape, and that hearing the correct response (which agrees with his own) will constitute an adequate reinforcement or reward of his effort. All of these assumptions are at best only partially true, and the teacher must keep in mind that the laboratory (at least as constructed and used at present) does not allow the teacher to relinquish his role as the person who is rewarding appropriate responses and correcting inappropriate ones.

In general, it must also be emphasized that the laboratory is a tool of instruction and that the tool should not be allowed to dominate and shape the instructional process as such. Thus, if it becomes very clear that a particular drill or activity is not benefiting the class (e.g., directions have been misunderstood, class is not sufficiently prepared for the drill) it is better to interrupt the activity than to let the laboratory session degenerate into a chaotic performance simply because a fixed amount of time had been mistakenly assigned to a specific laboratory activity.

4. The above-mentioned role of the laboratory as a tool must also determine its overall utilization. In general, the laboratory should be used *only when its utilization is required by the progress of the course.* Such use necessitates either extremely careful planning in the organization of the course or an amount of flexibility as to when and how long the laboratory should be used. There is little doubt that the latter is preferable since, even with the most careful planning, it is difficult to arrange classroom instruction in such a way that the availability of the laboratory will coincide with its most effective use. (It is for this reason, no doubt, that many schools are installing "Classroom laboratories" in which the teacher can switch at will from the classroom to the laboratory type of instruction.) At any rate, a topic that must be abandoned, an explanation which cannot be given, a drill which must be interrupted because it is time to go to the language laboratory—all of these not only result in a waste of time but also emphasize the lack of continuity between classroom and lab instruction.

What is true about the transition from classroom to laboratory instruction applies, of course, as well to the transition from lab to classroom and to the time devoted to laboratory instruction. There seems to be general agreement that the time that can be profitably spent on overlearning and reviewing material in the laboratory is fairly limited (perhaps an optimum of about twenty minutes). At this point we should emphasize again that this limited optimum duration applies only to the laboratory activities envisaged in this particular context and discussion and not necessarily to the flexible types of utilization described earlier (e.g., use of the laboratory as a center for programmed self-instruction). At any rate, the teacher should be in a position to interrupt laboratory activities if they no longer seem profitable (that is, when there are signs of student fatigue, boredom, confusion, etc.) and should not prolong drill activities simply because they were provided for in a predetermined schedule. Nor should the exigencies of a predetermined schedule force the teacher to take up in the laboratory certain types of activities (e.g., explanations, presentation of basic materials) which can be more profitably pursued in the classroom situation.

5. If, however, a superimposed rigidity in scheduling forces the teacher to spend more time in the laboratory than would be spent for the purpose of practice or overlearning, he must see to it that this time is spent as profitably as possible and not in repetitive types of exercises in which boredom and exhaustion lead not only to ever diminishing returns but also to creation of negative attitudes toward the lab experience as such. Activities like listening to short stories (based on familiar materials) followed by comprehension exercises, showing of pictures or films, filmstrips, playing of songs, etc. can be used to fill the scheduled laboratory period in a way which is interesting and at the same time reasonably profitable.

6. We have already stressed the point that laboratory activities must be completely integrated with classroom activities which precede and follow the laboratory session. Integration with the classroom activities which follow can be accomplished in various ways. Obviously, the laboratory drill can serve as the preparation for quizzes and tests to be taken during the following classroom session. Classroom activities can begin where the laboratory activity left off (e.g., materials or drills presented in the lab can be presented again and/or recombined in the classroom; if a short story or dialogue was drilled in the laboratory, the next class session can start with questions or discussions concerning the story or dialogue). In short, everything possible must be done in order to make it clear that the laboratory activity is an integral part of the course and essential to the total learning experience.

X. Making Homework Assignments

The teacher:

1. Chooses assignments designed to reinforce the learning which takes place in class.

    (a) Refrains from making assignments which force students onto unfamiliar ground.

    (b) Makes certain that the nature of the assignments necessitates active FL behavior on the part of the students.

2. Evaluates assignments in terms of the results achieved through the assignments rather than via physical evidence of their having been completed.

3. Clearly explains *what* is to be done and *how* it is to be done. (Uses class time, when necessary, to illustrate and practice procedures to be employed in accomplishing assignments.)

4. Makes assignments at appropriate time during the lesson. (Allows sufficient, but not excessive, time to explain expectations.)

5. Provides opportunity to confirm or correct assigned work as soon as possible.

    (a) Makes homework correction a class activity on most occasions.

    (b) Uses visual aids to facilitate correction (e.g., overhead projector, colored chalk).

    (c) Makes sure that each student is motivated to correct his homework carefully and conscientiously.

1. The main purpose of homework (at least at the first levels of instruction) is to reinforce learning which has already taken place in the classroom. Thus homework should, normally at least, represent an extention of classroom activity. In making assignments for homework, the teacher must keep in mind the simple facts that, on the one hand, the homework should represent some language activity on the part of the student while, on the other hand, the student will be working by himself so that errors will go uncorrected — at least until correction takes place in the classroom. (Immediate correction of homework could be possible only in special cases. For instance, the homework assignment is done in the language laboratory and consists of listening to tapes and records, or the student takes home specially designed "programmed" self-instructional materials.)

The normal homework assignment must, therefore, consist of exercises in which the student is not likely to make an unreasonable number of errors. The student must be on familiar ground, performing learning tasks that are active and useful and at the same time reasonably "safe." Some examples of such activities are:

(a) Writing out a drill that has already been performed orally.

(b) Continuing a drill (in spoken or written form) that has already been started in class.

(c) Making new sentences on the model of a sample sentence.

(d) Making new sentences out of a sample sentence by replacing words in the sentences with new words either supplied by the teacher or of the pupil's own choice.

As the student's ability in the foreign language increases and the amount of "control" in his language activities is generally relaxed, he must also receive more opportunity for freedom and creativity in his homework assignment. But even on those more advanced levels, the teacher must be careful to relax control gradually so that the homework assignment does not become an opportunity for making numerous uncontrollable errors. Exercises in writing "free composition" must be preceded by assignments in guided composition (in which the teacher tells the student just what to write about, what constructions to use, etc.). Homework that forces the student prematurely onto unfamiliar ground not only leads the student into numerous errors but also burdens the teacher with an unmanageable task of correction (and any written homework that goes uncorrected is of limited value, if any).

2. The tendency of many pupils is to think of homework as an end in itself rather than a means to an end. It is a specific task to be "gotten over with" so that other, perhaps more interesting and pleasant, occupations may be undertaken. Corollaries of this attitude are that the homework may not be done at all, that it may be done hastily without real involvement or effort to learn, that it may be copied from a classmate, etc. The teacher must do all in his power to counteract this attitude. He must make it

clear that the purpose of homework is learning experience and not the production of some physical realia (e.g., a sheet of paper with ten sentences written on it) to be brought along to the classroom. The best ways to impress this fact on the pupil are (a) not to give homework assignments which are obviously not designed to reinforce a learning experience, (b) to evaluate the homework in terms of the results achieved by it rather than in terms of the physical evidence of its completion. In other words, classroom activities, quizzes, tests, etc. should be structured in such a way that the homework presents a direct and meaningful preparation for the students. Only in the most advanced stages of instruction should homework as such be graded A, B, C, D, etc. (e.g., free composition, report on a book read outside of class, etc.).

This does not mean that the fact that homework is not done should go unnoticed, even on lower levels of instruction. It should be made clear to the student that the real "punishment" for not doing the homework is lower achievement than he would otherwise attain. Occasionally, as a result of the lack of grouping, there may indeed be the case of the rare student who can get all A's without doing any homework. Depending on other factors involved (general attitude of the student, his performance in other class activities) the teacher may let him "get away" without doing his homework or, better yet, provide some sort of special assignment.

3. Since the student doing his homework is on his own, the "what" and especially the "how" of the assignment must be very clearly explained. Again, laboratory homework and programmed, self-instructional materials are, of course, very specifically designed to control the way in which the student works when he is alone. In the normal homework situation, however, the teacher must provide very specific instructions in the classroom and, if necessary, model the procedure. To say: "Memorize the first four lines of a dialogue" may seem a very specific assignment, but it can be made more specific by saying: "Memorize the lines in the following way: Read the first line out

loud several times, then cover it; see whether you remember it; if you don't, say it a few more times out loud while reading; do not proceed to the second line until you know the first one ...." etc. An assignment like: "Make sentences of your own on the model of the following sentence" may have to be illustrated very carefully by taking class time to construct some sample sentences in the same way. One means of settling the "how" and "what" questions of homework assignment is to assign as homework the completion of an exercise started in the class (the written form of an exercise done audio-lingually, etc.).

4. Since the "how" and the "what" of the homework must be clearly explained, it is obvious that the homework assignment itself must be made at a time when these explanations are logically required by the progress of the lesson, and when there is sufficient time to give explanations and, if necessary, answer questions concerning the homework. Probably the most inappropriate time for making the assignment is the moment immediately before the end of the period, or the very end of the period itself. The last minutes of class can, perhaps, be used to remind the students of the assignment. The assignment itself should be made at the most appropriate time during the class period.

5. All written homework should be corrected. In conjunction with homework correction, we should remember that these simple principles of learning are applicable:
    (a) The correction should come as soon as possible.
    (b) Pupils' correct answers should be rewarded.
    (c) The incorrect items must be pointed out and the student must have the opportunity to formulate correct answers.
From these principles, it follows that homework should preferably be corrected the day after the assignment was made and that each student should correct his own work in such a way as to enable him to see which answers are correct and to rewrite correctly those which are incorrect.
In no case should homework be exchanged so that stu-

dents correct each other's assignments. Nor should class time be wasted by individual pupils putting sections of the homework on the board at the beginning of the class session. (This procedure leaves those who are not at the board either with nothing to do or with a different, distracting activity.) One effective way of correcting homework is for the teacher to put the required answers (section by section, sentence by sentence) on the board. Visual aids (colored chalk, underlining, etc.) can be used to draw the attention of the class to the critical points. Especially effective for the purpose of providing the correct model for the assignment is the overhead projector, since the answers can be written out by the teacher before the class and no class time at all is wasted in producing the corrections.

On the more advanced level of instruction this type of homework correction will, in many cases, be impossible. Free composition assignments must obviously be corrected individually by the teacher. (In the case of more controlled, "guided" composition, it is still possible to provide, as a result of classroom activity, one correct model which is used as a basis for audio-lingual activities such as questions and answers, discussion, etc.). Individual compositions which have been corrected should be rewritten by the pupil, and the teacher should check (or at least spot-check) the corrected work.

Whether correction of homework by the student is an activity undertaken at home (e.g., on the advanced level: rewriting of a free composition which has been corrected by the teacher) or an activity undertaken in class, the student must be motivated to correct his homework carefully and conscientiously. The student-corrected homework should be periodically checked by the teacher. This means that each student should be required to keep a special notebook or folder for his corrected homework. Such a folder or notebook can serve two useful purposes. It can be useful for review purposes, since the corrected homework will be a very graphic reminder of the correct answers, especially in those areas in which the student is most likely to make mistakes. Secondly, it can accord to homework (and homework correction) the status which it deserves as a useful learning experience.

XI. Testing

The teacher:
1. Gives frequent short quizzes.
2. Uses a variety of techniques to test the various skills.
3. Tests only after the class has been thoroughly prepared.
4. Makes sure the students understand the test items and procedures.
    (a) Gives clear and complete instructions for taking the test.
    (b) Monitors the test to provide additional clarification.
5. Provides feedback as soon as possible.
6. Uses information derived from item analysis and review of the test as a basis for making necessary changes in teaching and/or testing procedures.
7. Uses clearly defined criteria known to and understood by the class as the basis for grading tests.

Testing serves several purposes: it is necessary in order to establish the grades of the pupils; it may be necessary to provide motivation for learning; it is, most of all, useful as a diagnostic instrument. Testing tells the pupil which items have been learned and which ones need further review; it tells the teacher what the achievement of the class is, what parts of the material have been learned and taught well, what parts may have to be taught again or perhaps be taught differently.

1. No matter what particular purpose of testing one wishes to emphasize, the periodic, frequent, short quiz instead of (or at least in addition to) the large exam at the end of a longer time period is an *essential* part of the language course. When used for establishing the grade of the pupil, short quizzes remove the danger of attaching undue importance to a single performance influenced, per-haps, by unusual circumstances, and they will tend to reduce the amount of anxiety associated with the process of being examined. For the purpose of motivating the student to learn regularly and steadily, the long, compre-

hensive final examination is useless. It is even more useless for the purpose of providing feedback to either the pupil or the teacher. It establishes the outcome of a procedure which (at least within the same course) is no longer reversible. The final exam is not the time to find out that either the learning or the teaching process has gone astray.

2. It is not our intention to discuss in detail all the possible techniques of foreign language testing. Various books, manuals, etc. may be consulted for specific types of test items. However, some general principles will be emphasized:

(a) If we attach importance to all language skills (speaking, listening, reading, writing), then all skills must be tested.

(b) It is better to test any skill directly than indirectly (that is, by its correlation with another skill). The validity of any test diminishes as we rely on testing as a correlation with the skill tested rather than on testing the skill itself. Excessive reliance on a correlation may in fact upset the correlation itself.

(c) There may at times be a conflict between validity of a test and the requirement of ease of scoring. In general, the foreign language teacher should keep in mind that certain types of tests employed in widely used, nationally normed examinations are often influenced by the requirement of easy objective scoring, but are not necessarily the best models to be followed in preparing short classroom quizzes or tests.

(d) It is better to use a variety of techniques to test a skill than to rely constantly on just one technique. Reliance on just one technique may be unfair to the pupil who may have difficulty with that particular technique and may also ultimately influence the pupil to learn the material in just the way in which it is needed to do well in a specific type of response.

In demonstration of the above points:

(a) It is generally easier to test the passive skills than

the active ones. "True-false" or "Multiple choice"
techniques lend themselves very easily to testing
of either auditory or reading comprehension. As
a result, the teacher may be tempted to test the
passive skills and neglect the others, especially the
speaking skills. However, the neglect of testing
the speaking skill will inevitably de-emphasize
its importance in the eyes of the student. Thus,
short tests of individual pronunciation and ability
to speak (answer questions, react to pictures, etc.)
must be included in the testing procedure if speaking the language is to be one of the goals of
instruction.

(b) It is, of course, true that there is usually a very
high correlation between performances in the various skills, but the correlation does not provide
motivation to pursue and practice the skill which
is *not* being tested. In addition, the testing of
items which correlate with performance rather
than testing the performance itself can have ad-
verse results. To give a well-known example:
There is (normally, at least) a high correlation
between the ability to either speak or read and the
knowledge of vocabulary. At the same time, knowledge of vocabulary is not an end in itself. The constant use in the past of vocabulary tests on some
well-known standardized examinations resulted in
the stress on the learning of vocabulary as such
and produced students who knew vocabulary but
could neither speak nor read the language.

(c) The use of the correlation between knowledge of
vocabulary and reading on nationally used tests
is, of course, principally determined by one factor: ease of scoring. In general, the classroom
teacher would do well to keep in mind that ease of
scoring should not become a factor of overwhelm-
ing importance in making up short quizzes—at
least not at the expense of validity, and especially
not in the testing of the active skills. The best way

of testing speaking is to make the student speak. The best way of testing the student's knowledge of grammatical points in either spoken or written performance is to have the student say or write a sentence containing the particular point of grammar, and *not* to have him pick out one of four or five possible ways to complete a sentence.

3. The use of the test as a motivating as well as a diagnostic tool makes it mandatory that a quiz or test be given only after all of the material covered by the quiz has been thoroughly and clearly taught. The student should be (or should, at least, have had the opportunity to become) thoroughly familiar with all of the materials as well as the testing procedures themselves. This means that the testing procedure as such should be carefully explained, preferably before the quiz or exam is given, and should, whenever possible, be closely related to the *teaching* procedure (e.g., if the teaching procedure has relied heavily on answers to pictorial cues, on making affirmative sentences negative, on changing tenses of verbs at agreed-upon signals, on replacing nouns with pronouns, etc., then the same procedure should also be used in the construction of test or quiz items). There is no justification for introducing new, unusual procedures or test items which test the student's ability to grasp the testing procedure rather than his knowledge of the language.

4. From what is said above, it follows that the instructions for taking the test, and the test items themselves must be perfectly clear. If the teacher feels that it is preferable to use the foreign language in giving his instructions, then he must be especially careful to use only familiar, recurrent types of test items and to explain the test items themselves very carefully, perhaps in class sessions preceding the administration of the quiz or exam. During the test itself, the teacher should also be on hand to provide clarification as to what is required. He can show, at the same time, interest in the performance of each student, reassure the insecure students, perhaps walk up

and down and ask individuals whether they clearly understand what they are supposed to do. (This procedure will, of course, also allow the teacher to prevent possible cheating without casting him too obviously in the role of a policeman.)

5. The role of the test as a diagnostic tool requires that it be corrected and returned to the student as soon as possible. If the student is to "learn from the test," then he should receive correction of his wrong responses (and confirmation of the right ones) as quickly as possible. In the case of individual speaking and/or pronunciation tests, correction and confirmation is, of course, immediate. Written quizzes can be discussed and corrected in the class period following the quiz. Some teachers prefer to give the correction immediately after the quiz is taken. This procedure has the advantage of immediate correction and confirmation, but the disadvantage that the student cannot correct his own mistakes, at least not if the quiz is to be used to establish a grade. (The temptation to change the answer is too great to be resisted.) Some teachers follow the practice of having students exchange papers for correction. This procedure neither removes the temptation to make changes (this time on the exam paper of a friend) nor does it give the individual the chance to have direct confirmation or correction of his own answers. Thus, for any exam used for purposes of grading, the best procedure is correction of the exam by the teacher, but in such a way that mistakes are noted on the paper but no correct response is provided. Then, during the next session of the class, the correct answers are provided (on the blackboard or overhead projector) and the students write out the correct answers. Just as with corrected homework, corrected quizzes should not be thrown away but be kept in a special notebook or folder by each individual student.

6. Each quiz tests not only the students, but, in a very real sense, the teacher as well. It gives him the opportunity to evaluate himself and his techniques. Thus, a teacher must consider the results of any exam first of all from the

point of view of whether the class as a whole has reached satisfactory achievement. Then the specific test items should be examined with some care. If certain test items were missed consistently by the majority of the students, then the specific material tested by those items was perhaps badly or inefficiently taught. If the item is missed by the better students or missed randomly by good and bad students alike, then the test item itself was unreliable and badly constructed. Thus, the test will give the teacher clear indications whether the teaching or the testing procedure or both need modification. A teacher, especially a beginning teacher, may find it useful to keep a "log" of his quizzes and tests in order to modify his own performance as the result of the feedback received.

7. The purposes of providing feedback and motivation can be interfered with quite seriously if the student perceives the test or the grading system as "unfair" and is allowed to come to the conclusion that the reason for a low grade or wrong response can be found with the teacher rather than with his own performance. The teacher must, therefore, make sure that the students know exactly not only what their mistakes are but also the criteria on which the grades are based. The teacher should communicate very briefly how much each mistake (or type of mistake) counted, how much value was assigned to each part of the examination and within which brackets specific grades were assigned.

Part III. Micro-Lessons

As stated in the introduction to this volume, the micro-teaching lesson is the experience in which all the other elements which make up the training of the teacher find their practical application. What goes then into the make-up of the micro-lesson is the teacher's understanding of the linguistic principles involved (Part I), his knowledge of and fluency in the language (Part II), and his grasp of essential aspects of methodology (the performance criteria of Part II).

In Part III of this training syllabus we shall thus describe a few samples of micro-lessons — or rather the planning which should go into those micro-lessons. For it is essential that micro-teaching lessons be *real* lessons — and that micro-teaching be considered as *real* teaching. It is a scaled-down model of reality — not play-acting. The model lessons described here can be video-taped or simply taught "live" by the supervisor or master-teacher. In the video-taping as well as in the live performance, it may, of course, become necessary to depart from the planning — from the "script" which is envisaged in the planning of the lessons. Such departures which are forced upon the experienced teacher and which are likely to be within the scope of the performance criteria of Part II should by no means be avoided. They can themselves become unplanned models of specific performance criteria. At any rate, it is by far preferable to have such unpredictable departures from planning in the model lessons than to put on an obviously agreed-upon stage performance. Flexibility and the ability to draw upon some of the performance criteria in unpredictable situations are themselves essential skills which are in need of demonstration in a natural setting.

The students chosen for the micro-lessons should preferably be slightly *ahead* of the level and material itself. Numbers after the number of the lesson (½, 1, 1½) refer to recommended levels of their preparation.

INDEX TO MICRO-LESSONS

Micro-lesson	Performance Criteria and Linguistic Basis
Phonology	
1. Teaching the fricative sounds [ƀ, đ] as opposed to the stop sounds [b, d].	IV, V, II, I; 3, 4
2a. Pronunciation of the alveolar "flap" /r/.	IV, V, II, I; 6
2b. Pronunciation of the alveolar "flap" /r/. (assuming the intervocalic [đ] has been taught).	IV, V, II, I; 6
3. Pronunciation of trill /r̄/ using /r/ − /r̄/ contrast.	IV, II, I; 6
4. Avoidance of substitution of English diphthongal vowels.	IV, V, II, I; 8, 9
5. Testing auditory discrimination of English diphthongs and Spanish vowels.	IV, V, II, I; 8, 9
6. Establishing sound-symbol relationship: ⟨s⟩, ⟨c⟩, ⟨z⟩ = /s/.	V, IV, II, I, VIII; 5
7. Teaching distinction between second person singular forms: use of ⟨tú⟩ as opposed to the use of ⟨usted⟩.	III, II, I; 13, 14
8. Teaching regular plural formations: definite articles, nouns and adjectives.	III, II, I; 12, 17, 18
9. Teaching the shortened vs. longer forms of certain adjectives in Spanish (apocopation): their allomorphic difference and syntactic position.	III, II, I; 18, 19, 52, 53, 60

Micro-lesson	Performance Criteria and Linguistic Basis
10. Teaching the direct object pronouns: ⟨lo⟩, ⟨la⟩ (third person singular inanimate).	VIII, III, II, I; 14, 15
11. Teaching the imperfect tense: the initial presentation of /er/ and /ir/ verbs.	III, II, I; 19, 20, 30, 31, 32, 33
12. Teaching the imperfect tense: complementary practice of /er/ and /ir/ verbs.	VIII, III, II, I; 19, 20, 30, 31, 32, 33
13. Teaching the preterite tense: the initial presentation of /ar/ verbs.	III, II, I; 19, 20, 30-33
14. Teaching the preterite tense: complementary practice of /ar/ verbs.	VIII, III, II, I; 19, 20, 31-33
15. Teaching Class 1, /e/ to /ie/ change, of radical changing verbs: initial presentation.	VIII, III, II, I; 23, 24
15a. Related homework assignment.	X, III, II, I; 24
16. Teaching Class 1, /e/ to /ie/ change of radical changing verbs: complementary practice.	X, III, II, I; 24
17. Test on Class 1, /e/ to /ie/ change of radical changing verbs.	XI, III, II, I; 24
18. Teaching the imperfect-preterite contrast.	III, I; 26, 31-33
19. Use of the subjunctive in noun clauses: restricted to examples using verbs of doubt and emotion in independent clauses.	III, II, I; 35
20. Test on the use of the subjunctive in noun clauses; restricted to examples using verbs of doubt and emotion in independent clauses.	XI; 35
21. Teaching the subject-object reversal: gustar, parecer, encantar, faltar.	III, II, I; 43, 44
22. Teaching the lack of Spanish-English pattern correspondence in expressions of weather.	VIII, III, II, I; 50, 51
23. Teaching personal ⟨a⟩.	III, II, I; 52
24. Teaching the reflexive construction for use in impersonal expressions.	III, II, I; 47, 48
25. Teaching ⟨conocer/saber⟩ distinction: different lexical items correspond to a given English item.	III, II, I; 53-55
26. Testing the correct use of ⟨saber⟩ and ⟨conocer⟩.	XI, III, II, I; 53-55
27. Teaching false cognates.	VIII, II; 59

Micro-lesson	Performance Criteria and Linguistic Basis
28. Sensitizing students to semantic difference found in the use of the predicate adjective with ⟨ser⟩ and ⟨estar⟩.	VII, II, I; 57-59
29. Teaching a short reading passage and utilizing it for conversational practice.	VI
30. Use of the tape recorder in the introduction of a new dialogue.	XI, III, II, I
31. Teaching a song.	VII

MICRO-LESSON 1A. (1/2)

Goal: Teaching of the fricative [ƀ] as opposed to the stop [b]: Teaching of the fricative [đ] as opposed to the stoɉ [d].

Linguistic Basis: Refer to pp. 3, 4

Performance Criteria:

    Used in planning: IV

    Additional references: V, II, I

                [b]−[ƀ]

OUTLINE OF LESSON:

A. Teacher models words:

	voz	la voz
	hambre	abre
	viene	no viene
	bajo	abajo
Teacher:	voz	la voz	(signals repetition)
Class:	voz	la voz
Teacher:	hambre	abre	(signals repetition)
Class:	hambre	abre
Teacher:	viene	no viene	(signals repetition)
Class:	viene	no viene
Teacher:	bajo	abajo	(signals repetition)
Class:	bajo	abajo

B. Teacher asks: ¿Quién nota una diferencia? Who sees a difference? Teacher can listen to explanations offered and then explain that the sound /b/ in initial position or following ⟨m or n⟩ is pronounced as in English, but, in any other position, it is produced by keeping the lips slightly apart permitting a continuous passage of air.

C. Teacher models and shows the difference:

Teacher:	voz	la voz	(signals repetition)
Class:	voz	la voz	
Teacher:	hambre	abre	(signals repetition)
Class:	hambre	abre	
Teacher:	viene	no viene	(signals repetition)
Class:	viene	no viene	
Teacher:	bajo	abajo	(signals repetition)
Class:	bajo	abajo	

D. The teacher follows the above procedure (part C) with individual students, especially with those who seemed to have difficulty during choral repetition.

E. Teacher writes the various expressions on the board or uses large poster cards (see example) and then models contrasting words for class to repeat. At this time, the teacher explains the principle: the orthographic ⟨v⟩ follows the same pronunciation rules as the orthographic ⟨b⟩. The ⟨v⟩ has no individual sound corresponding to it.

b	ƀ
voz	la voz
hambre	abre
viene	no viene
bajo	abajo

F. Teacher asks students to read the words which have been written on the board (or on poster cards). Teacher rewards correct pronunciation and corrects errors. Teacher also calls on individual students to read the words.

[d]—[đ]

(It is assumed that the Spanish stop [d]—English stop [d] contrast has been taught. The same procedure used for the [b—ƀ] contrast is followed for the [d—đ] contrast.)

MICRO-LESSON 1B

OUTLINE OF LESSON:

A. Teacher models words:

donde	adónde
el dios	adiós
un dios	una diosa
día	ese día

Teacher:	donde	adónde	(signals repetition)
Class:	donde	adónde	
Teacher:	el dios	adiós	(signals repetition)
Class:	el dios	adiós	
Teacher:	un dios	una diosa	(signals repetition)
Class:	un dios	una diosa	
Teacher:	día	ese día	(signals repetition)
Class:	día	ese día	

B. Teacher asks: ¿Quién nota una diferencia? Who sees a difference? Teacher can listen to explanations offered and then, explains that the sound /d/ in initial position or following ⟨m, n, l⟩ is produced by placing the tip of the tongue behind the teeth. In any other position, the /d/ is pronounced by placing the tongue between the teeth.

C. Teacher models and shows the difference:

Teacher:	donde	adónde	(signals repetition)
Class:	donde	adónde	
Teacher:	el dios	adiós	(signals repetition)
Class:	el dios	adiós	
Teacher:	un dios	una diosa	(signals repetition)
Class:	un dios	una diosa	
Teacher:	día	ese día	(signals repetition)
Class:	día	ese día	

D. The teacher follows the above procedure (part C) with individual students, especially with those who seemed to have difficulty during choral repetition.

E. Teacher writes the various expressions on the board or uses large poster cards (see example) and, then, models contrasting words for class to repeat.

d	đ
donde	adónde
el dios	adiós
un dios	una diosa
día	ese día

F. Teacher asks students to read the words which have been written on the board (or on poster cards). Teacher rewards correct pronunciation and corrects errors. Teacher also calls on individual students to read the words.

MICRO-LESSON 2A. (1/2)

Goal: Pronunciation of the alveolar "flap" /r/.

Linguistic Basis: refer to p. 6.

Performance Criteria:

Used in planning: IV

Additional references: I, II, V

OUTLINE OF LESSON:

A. Teacher: while drilling the dialogue, the teacher models sentence:

"María y yo queremos invitarle al parque." bis

Teacher signals repetition and uses the "backward buildup."

Teacher: invitarle al parque

Class: invitarle al parque

Teacher: queremos invitarle al parque

Class: queremos invitarle al parque

Teacher: María y yo queremos invitarle al parque

Class: María y yo queremos invitarle al parque bis

B. Teacher explains the purpose of the lesson. A medial ⟨r⟩ is a "flap" /r/. A close substitute sound in English is Be*tt*y, la*dd*er when these double consonants are pronounced rapidly. This explanation is given in English.

Teacher models: Be*tt*y la*dd*er Pa*tt*y (signals repetition)

Class: Be*tt*y la*dd*er Pa*tt*y

Teacher: Be*tt*y pe*r*o (signals repetition)

Class: Be*tty* pe*r*o
Teacher: Pa*tty* pa*r*a   (signals repetition)
Class: Pa*tty* pa*r*a

C. Teacher asks for individual repetition by pointing to individual students. Teacher acts as model.
    Teacher: María ... María
    Student: María ... María
    Teacher: queremos ... queremos
    Student: queremos ... queremos, etc.
    Teacher rewards correct responses; does not reward incorrect responses.

D. Teacher varies individual and choral repetition of the words and phrase being taught.

E. Teacher writes the phrase on the board, underlining the letter corresponding to the sound /r/.
    "Ma*r*ía y yo que*r*emos invita*r*le al parque."
    Teacher: pronounces the word of the underlined sound while pointing to it.
    Class: repeats (or individual repetition; both choral and individual repetition may be used).

MICRO-LESSON 2B. (1/2)

Goal: Pronunciation of alveolar "flap" /r/ (assuming intervocalic [đ] has been taught).
Linguistic Basis: Refer to p. 6.
Performance Criteria:
    Used in planning: IV
    Additional references: I,II, V

OUTLINE OF LESSON:

A. Teacher: while drilling the dialogue, the teacher models sentence:
    "La cara del toro es de cera."   bis
    The teacher uses the "backward buildup" to facilitate repetition.
    Teacher: ... es de cera   (signals repetition)
    Class: es de cera
    Teacher: ... del toro es de cera   (signals repetition)
    Class: ... del toro es de cera

Teacher: ... La cara del toro es
de cera   (signals repetition)
Class: La cara del toro es
de cera   bis

B. The teacher explains purpose of the lesson. A medial
⟨r⟩ is a "flap" /r/. A close substitute sound in English
is Be*tt*y, la*dd*er when double consonants are pronounced rapidly. The following words are read to
the students in order to help them perceive the
difference between the English and the Spanish
sounds.

English	*Spanish*
serra	cera
Taurus	toro
Cara	cara

C. Teacher signals choral repetition using English /d/ —
Spanish /r/ contrast:

Written form	*English /d/*	*Spanish /r/*
cara	caddy	/cara/
toro	Betty	/toro/
cera	Patty	/sera/

D. Teacher signals choral repetition using Spanish [đ]
—Spanish /r/ contrast:

/cađa/	/cara/
/tođo/	/toro/
/sеđa/	/sera/

E. Teacher signals individual repetition by pointing to
individual students. Teacher acts as model.

/cađa/	/cara/
/tođo/	/toro/
/sеđa/	/sera/

F. Choral repetition followed by individual repetition of
entire phrase:
"La cara del toro es de cera."

G. Teacher writes the phrase on the board, underlining
the letter corresponding to the sound /r/.
"La ca*r*a del to*r*o es de ce*r*a."

Teacher: Pronounces the underlined sound while
pointing to it.
Class: repeats.
Teacher uses both choral and individual repetition.

MICRO-LESSON 3. (1/2)

Goal: Pronunciation of trill /r̄/ using /r/ – /r̄/ contrast.
Linguistic Basis: Refer to p. 6
Performance Criteria:
     Used in planning: IV
     Additional references: I, II

OUTLINE OF LESSON:

A. Teacher: while drilling dialogue models sentence:
     ¡Mira! Se ríe de la cara del perro.
     /mira   se r̄ie đe la kara đel per̄o/
     To facilitate imitation and repetition, the teacher uses
     the "backward buildup". Teacher models:

Teacher:	. . . el perro	(signals repetition)
Class:	el perro	
Teacher:	. . . la cara del perro	(signals repetition)
Class:	la cara del perro	
Teacher:	. . . se ríe de la cara del perro	(signals repetition)
Class:	se ríe de la cara del perro	
Teacher:	. . . Mira, se ríe de la cara del perro	(signals repetition)
Class:	Mira, se ríe de la cara del perro	

B. Teacher explains the purpose of the lesson:
     – continued practice of the medial /r/
     – learn pronunciation of trill by putting tip of the
       tongue against the roof of the mouth and trying
       to let it vibrate.
     Teacher asks students whether or not they can hear the
     difference between the medial /r/ and the trill /r̄/.
     They are to raise their hands when the hear the trill
     /r̄/. (Al oir el sonido de la /r̄/, levanten la mano.)
     Teacher: pero . . . perro; carro . . . caro; morro . . . moro

C. Teacher gives the example and then signals choral
     repetition for the following exercise:

Teacher:	pero	perro
Class:	pero	perro

Teacher:	caro	carro
Class:	caro	carro
Teacher:	moro	morro
Class:	moro	morro

Teacher gives example ... pero — perro ... and signals individual repetition especially from those who seemed to experience difficulty in choral repetition.

MICRO-LESSON 4. (1/2)

Goal: Avoidance of substitution of English diphthongal vowels.

Linguistic Basis: Refer to pp. 8, 9

Performance Criteria:

    Used in planning: IV

    Additional references: V, II, I

OUTLINE OF LESSON:

A. Teacher models sounds and explains that the first word in each pair will be English and the second word will be Spanish. The purpose is for the student to hear the difference between English and Spanish. Later, the teacher will explain the difference in more detail.

English	*Spanish*
me	mi
tea	ti
say	se
may	me
low	lo
Sue	su

Teacher:	me	mi
Class:	me	mi
Teacher:	tea	ti
Class:	tea	ti
Teacher:	say	se
Class:	say	se
Teacher:	may	me
Class:	may	me
Teacher:	low	lo

	English	*Spanish*
Class:	low	lo
Teacher:	Sue	su
Class:	Sue	su

B. The above exercise is repeated, using individual students especially those who seemed to have trouble with choral repetition.

C. Taking the words of the previous exercise, the teacher explains that the students are to select the Spanish word. Example: say ... say ... se ... say. Once the teacher has pronounced all four words, the students are to raise their hands and say "uno" if the Spanish word was the first said, "dos" if it was the second, etc. Students are to wait until called upon.

D. Teacher: ¿Qué diferencia notan ustedes entre la palabra en inglés y la palabra en español? What difference do you hear between the English word and the Spanish word? Teacher listens to explanations and then explains that the Spanish vowels sound shorter than the English vowels and that they are not diphthongized as they are in English.

E. Teacher repeats previous drill, using both choral and individual repetition emphasizing the contrast which has just been explained.

F. Teacher now writes familiar words containing the Spanish vowels on the board and asks the class or individuals to read them.

MICRO-LESSON 5. (1/2)

Goal: Testing auditory discrimination of English Diphthongs and Spanish vowels.
Linguistic Basis: Refer to pp. 8, 9
Performance Criteria:
  Used in planning: XI, IV

OUTLINE OF LESSON:

Teacher asks students to take a sheet of paper and a pencil. Students will be given several pairs of words from which they must select a Spanish word. Each pair will

contain one English word and one Spanish word. If the
Spanish word is the first word in the pair, the students are
to write 1; if it is the second, they are to write 2.

The following pairs may be used for the test. For the
purposes of a unified format, the English will be listed first
and then the Spanish. The teacher administering the test
must alternate the pairs.

English /iy/	*Spanish /i/*
me	mi
tea	ti
see	sí
bee	vi
Dee	di
knee	ni
English /uw/	*Spanish /u/*
too	tú
taboo	tabú
Cuckoo	Cucú (lady's nickname)
Sue	su
English /ow/	*Spanish /o/*
no	no
low	lo
cocoa	coco
dose	dos
coal	col
English /e/	*Spanish /e/*
mess	mes
Tess	tez
Bess	vez
Ben	ven
ten	ten
den	den
English /ey/	*Spanish /e/*
day	de
say	se
lay	le
may	me
Fay	fe
Kay	que
bay	ve

Diphthongs:

English /ey/	*Spanish* /ey/
lay	ley
base	veis
English /ay/	*Spanish* /ay/
eye	hay
English /oy/	*Spanish* /oy/
soy	soy
boy	voy
English /aw/	*Spanish* /aw/
chow	llegado (llegao, *as pronounced in popular speech*)

MICRO-LESSON 6. (1/2)

Goal: Establishing sound-symbol relationship: ⟨s⟩, ⟨c⟩, ⟨z⟩ = /s/

Linguistic Basis: Refer to p. 5

Performance Criteria:

Used in planning: V

Additional references: IV, II, I, VIII

OUTLINE OF LESSON:

A. Teacher models:

Los zapatos azules cuestan cinco pesos.

Teacher uses backward buildup and signals repetition:

Teacher: . . . cuestan cinco pesos

Class: . . . cuestan cinco pesos

Teacher: Los zapatos azules cuestan cinco pesos.

Class: Los zapatos azules cuestan cinco pesos.

While drilling the sentence, the teacher points to blue shoes (or a picture of blue shoes). The teacher can also write the number 5 on the board.

B. The teacher uses the above sentence for individual repetition. After, to insure that all students understand the sentence, the teacher asks: ¿Qué quiere decir esta frase? What does this sentence mean? The teacher listens to explanations and then gives English meaning.

C. The teacher writes the sentence on the board underlining (in colored chalk if possible) the sounds in the
words corresponding to /s/.

Los zapatos azules cuestan cinco pesos.

The students repeat the sentence while the teacher
points to the words. The teacher explains that in
Latin America and in the south of Spain, the letters
⟨s⟩, ⟨z⟩ and ⟨c⟩ before ⟨e⟩ and⟨i⟩ correspond to the
sound /s/. The teacher also explains that in the other
parts of Spain, the ⟨z⟩ and the ⟨c⟩ when followed by
⟨i⟩ and ⟨e⟩ is pronounced /Ө/. The students should
know this in order to understand the pronunciation
of the majority of Spaniards. At present, the class will
deal with ⟨c⟩, ⟨s⟩, and ⟨z⟩ corresponding to /s/.

D. The teacher asks the students to copy the sentence from
the board, pronouncing the words to themselves
as they write them. The students repeat the sentence
with the teacher.

E. The teacher erases the sentence from the board and
dictates it to the students. The teacher then rewrites
the sentence on the board in order to give the students the opportunity of correcting their errors.

Micro-lesson 7. (1/2)

Goal: Teaching distinction between second person singular forms; use of ⟨tú⟩ as opposed to the use of
⟨usted⟩.

Linguistic Basis: Refer to pp. 13, 14

Performance Criteria:

Used in planning: III

Additional references: I and II

Outline of lesson:

A. Teacher models:

	Yo hablo español.	(points to herself) bis (signals repetition)
Class:	Yo hablo español.	
Teacher:	Tú hablas español.	(points to 1 student) bis (signals repetition)

Class: Tú hablas español.

Teacher asks: ¿Qué significa: Yo hablo español? ¿Qué significa: Tú hablas español? Teacher insures that all students are aware of the English meaning.

B. Teacher: ¿Tú hablas español? (changes intonation pattern denoting question and points to student while asking question. Teacher indicates English meaning for clarification purposes.)

Student: Sí, yo hablo español. (Teacher helps student with first answer and uses English for clarification.)

Teacher to next student: ¿Tú hablas español?

Student: Sí, yo hablo español. (Teacher follows same procedure with each individual student.)

C. Teacher says to one student: Ask your neighbor if he speaks Spanish.

Student turns to neighbor: ¿Tú hablas español?

Neighbor: Sí, yo hablo español.

In this manner, the teacher has established chain drill which is continued with each student. Teacher directs chain drill by verbal cue or hand signal.

D. Teacher: Él habla español. (teacher points to male student) (signals repetition) bis

Class: Él habla español.

Teacher: Ella habla español. (teacher points to a girl) (signals repetition) bis

Class: Ella habla español.

Teacher: Él habla español. (teacher points to individual student signalling repetition)

Teacher: Ella habla español. (teacher points to individual student signalling repetition) (teacher calls on all students for individual repetition)

E. Teacher asks a female student: ¿Él habla español?
   While asking a female student the above question, the
   teacher points to a male student. Teacher also indi-
   cates English meaning for clarification purposes.
   Student: Sí, él habla (teacher helps student with
              español.   first answer)
   Teacher asks a male student: ¿Ella habla español?
   While asking a male student the above question, the
   teacher points to a female student. Teacher also indi-
   cates English meaning for clarification purposes.
   Student: Sí, ella habla (teacher helps student with
              español.   first answer)
   Teacher uses the above procedure with other students
   in the class.

F. Teacher asks one student: Ask me if I speak English.
   Student may say: ¿Tú hablas español? Teacher then
   explains to student that although he learned the pre-
   vious material well, in speaking to adults he must
   use ⟨usted⟩ form. Structural explanation for this form
   will be given *after* the form is introduced. Examples:
   Teacher says to one student: Ask me if I speak Spanish.
   Student should ask: ¿Usted habla español?
   If not, the teacher should indicate the correct form
   to student: ¿Usted habla español?
   Teacher to next student: Ask me if I speak Spanish.
   Student should ask: ¿Usted habla español?
   Teacher follows this procedure with each individual
   student repeating procedure with those who have
   previously given incorrect answers. It is suggested
   that the teacher reward each correct answer by verbal
   acknowledgement, nodding, smiling, etc.

G. Teacher can ask students if they can figure out the
   difference between ⟨tú⟩ and ⟨usted⟩. Then, teacher
   explains that in Spanish, the ⟨tú⟩ form is an informal
   form used when speaking to family and friends.
   ⟨Usted⟩ is the formal form used with adults, supe-
   riors or persons of slight acquaintance. ⟨Usted⟩
   takes the same verb form as ⟨él⟩ and ⟨ella⟩.

H. Teacher writes the forms on the board and goes over
   them orally with the students.

MICRO-LESSON 8. (1/2)

Goal: Teaching regular plural formations: definite articles, nouns and adjectives.

Linguistic Basis: Refer to pp. 12, 17, 18

Performance Criteria:

    Used in planning: III

    Additional references: I and II

OUTLINE OF LESSON:

A. Teacher models sentences:

    La falda es corta. El vestido es largo.

        (Teacher points to a skirt worn by a female stu-
dent and also a dress.)

    Las faldas son cortas. Los vestidos son largos.

        (Teacher indicates by hand motions that "corto"
means short and "largo" means long.)

Teacher models:	La falda es corta.	(signals repetition) bis
Class:	La falda es corta.	
Teacher:	El vestido es largo.	(signals repetition) bis
Class:	El vestido es largo.	
Teacher:	Las faldas son cortas.	(signals repetition) bis
Class:	Las faldas son cortas.	
Teacher:	Los vestidos son largos.	(signals repetition) bis
Class:	Los vestidos son largos.	

B. Teacher uses these exercises for individual repetition.
Teacher models sentences and then points to individual signalling repetition.

C. Teacher writes each pair of sentences on board (see
example) and asks class to look for obvious similarities.

    La falda es corta.

    Las faldas son cortas.

    - - - -

    El vestido es largo.

Los vestidos son largos.

Once students have volunteered answers, teacher can explain that the top sentence in each group is the singular form whereas the one below is its corresponding plural. Lines showing the plural endings should then be drawn as such:

La falda es corta.

La|s falda|s son corta|s.

- - - -

El vestido es largo.

Los vestido|s son largo|s.

A simple explanation then follows. In forming the plural of the feminine article and nouns and adjectives ending in vowels, one adds ⟨s⟩. The plural of ⟨el⟩ is ⟨los⟩. It is assumed that students have learned the verb ⟨ser⟩.

D. To test the comprehension of the above material, the teacher writes the following or other comparable sentences on the board and asks students to form the plurals. The teacher writes the answers when given by the students.

Teacher writes: El libro es grande.
Student: Los libros son grandes.
Teacher writes: La puerta es pequeña.
Student: Las puertas son pequeñas.

- - - -

Teacher writes: El carro es verde.
Student: Los carros son verdes.
Teacher writes: La silla es roja.
Student: Las sillas son rojas.

E. Teacher conducts oral drill asking students to change the following sentences from singular to plural. Individual students are to raise their hands to answer.

Teacher	*Student*
El muchacho es alto.	Los muchachos son altos.
La chica es bonita.	Las chicas son bonitas.
La novia es guapa.	Las novias son guapas.
El sombrero es nuevo.	Los sombreros son nuevos.

Teacher	*Student*
La casa es vieja.	Las casas son viejas.
¿Es ella la chica inteligente?	¿Son ellas las chicas inteligentes?
Su hermana está enferma.	Sus hermanas están enfermas.
¿Quiere usted el gato amarillo?	¿Quiere usted los gatos amarillos?

Micro-lesson 9, (1)

Goal: Teaching the shortened vs. longer forms of certain adjectives in Spanish (apocopation): their allomorphic difference and syntactic position.

Linguistic Basis: Refer to pp. 18, 19, 52, 53, 60

Performance Criteria:
   Used in planning: III
   Additional references: I, II

Outline of lesson:

A. Teacher models:

Es un mal profesor.	Es un profesor malo.
Era un buen niño.	Era un niño bueno.
Está en el primer piso.	Está en el piso primero.
Es un gran hombre.[1]	Es un hombre grande.[1]
No hay ningún hombre.	No hay hombre ninguno.
¿No hay algún plato?	No hay plato alguno.

Teacher models each pair of sentences twice; signals choral repetition, then individual repetition.

B. Each of the above is used in question form by changing the intonation.

Teacher asks: ¿Es un mal profesor?
   Teacher points at one student, indicating an answer is expected. At first, the teacher should help the students until the pattern of the drill is established.
Student: Sí, es un mal profesor.
Teacher: ¿Es un profesor malo?
Student: Sí, es un mal profesor.

C. The teacher explains structural concept: the above adjectives may be used before and after nouns in identical constructions.

    a) when placed before the noun, they lose the final ⟨o⟩ but when placed after the noun, they retain it: algún — alguno; buen — bueno; mal — malo; primer — primero; ningún — ninguno

    b) when placed before the noun, they lose the final syllable but when placed after the noun, they retain it: gran — grande

The following adjectives are also apocopated but they are not interchangeable in identical constructions: un — uno (a); tercer — tercero (a); cien — ciento (b).

D. The teacher uses transformation drill. As teacher gives one form (cue), the student transforms it.

Teacher cues	*Student*
Es un mal profesor.	Es un profesor malo.
Era un buen niño.	Era un niño bueno.
Está en el piso primero.	Está en el primer piso.

E. The teacher uses other sentences using these interchangeable adjectives in order to check student grasp of the material. The teacher can include sentences of her own also.

Teacher cues	*Student*
Hay un mal olor.	Hay un olor malo.
Es un buen libro.	Es un libro bueno.
Es una gran persona.[1]	Es una persona grande.[1]
No hay ningún paraguas.	No hay paraguas ninguno.

MICRO-LESSON 10. (1)

Goal: Teaching the direct object pronouns: ⟨lo⟩, ⟨la⟩ (3rd person singular inanimate).

Linguistic Basis: Refer to pp. 14, 15

Performance Criteria:

    Used in planning: III, VIII

    Additional references: I, II

---

[1] A change of meaning occurs here: *gran* refers to the virtue of magnanimity or to renown; *grande* refers to physical size.

OUTLINE OF LESSON:

A. Teacher models each pair of patterns; students repeat.

Traigo el libro.	Lo traigo.
Traigo el cuaderno.	Lo traigo.
Traigo la cartera.	La traigo.
Traigo la pluma.	La traigo.

B. Teacher models each pair and points to individual students to repeat.

C. Teacher explains that:

    1) a masculine inanimate object noun can be replaced by the direct object pronouns as in the sentence just learned:

       Traigo el libro.   Lo traigo.

       ⟨Libro⟩ is the masculine inanimate object; ⟨lo⟩ is the direct object pronoun which replaces it.

    2) a feminine inanimate object can be replaced by the direct object pronoun, as in the sentence just learned:

       Traigo la cartera.   La traigo.

D. Teacher uses the above sentences and others in the following substitution drills:

  1. Teacher gives example:

Traigo el libro.	Lo traigo.
Teacher:	*Students:*
Traigo el libro.	Lo traigo.
Traigo el cuaderno.	Lo traigo.
Traigo el lápiz.	Lo traigo.
Traigo el examen.	Lo traigo.
Traigo el periódico.	Lo traigo.

  2. Teacher gives example:

Traigo la cartera.	La traigo.
Teacher:	*Students:*
Traigo la cartera.	La traigo.
Traigo la pluma.	La traigo.
Traigo la almohada.	La traigo.
Traigo la blusa.	La traigo.
Traigo la servilleta.	La traigo.

3. Substitution Drill.

Traigo la pluma.	La traigo.
Traigo el automóvil.	Lo traigo.
Traigo la sartén.	La traigo.
Traigo la blusa.	La traigo.
Traigo el periódico.	Lo traigo.

E. Teacher writes one example using masculine object and one example using feminine object:

Traigo el libro.	Lo traigo.
Traigo la pluma.	La traigo.

Teacher points to ⟨lo⟩ and explains once again that ⟨lo⟩ is the direct object pronoun which can replace a masculine inanimate object whereas ⟨la⟩ (teacher points to ⟨la⟩) is the direct object pronoun which can replace a feminine inanimate object.

F. Question-Answer Drill

Teacher asks individual students questions eliciting response using direct object.

Teacher: ¿Tienes el libro?
Student: (teacher's help may be needed)
Sí, lo tengo.
Teacher: ¿Tienes la pluma?
Student: Sí, la tengo.
Teacher: ¿Tienes el examen?
Student: Sí, lo tengo.
Teacher: ¿Tienes la blusa?
Student: Sí, la tengo.
Teacher: ¿Tienes la sartén?
Student: Sí, la tengo.

MICRO-LESSON 11. (1 1/2)

Goal: Teaching of the imperfect tense: the initial presentation of /er/ and /ir/ verbs.
Linguistic Basis: Refer to pp. 19, 20, 30-33
Performance Criteria:
Used in planning: III
Additional references: I, II

Outline of lesson:

A. Teacher models:

Cuando yo era niño, vivíamos cerca de la ciudad donde mi padre tenía negocios.[1]

Teacher signals repetition using backward buildup:

... donde mi padre tenía negocios

Class: ... donde mi padre tenía negocios

Teacher: ... vivíamos cerca de la ciudad donde mi padre tenía negocios

Class: ... vivíamos cerca de la ciudad donde mi padre tenía negocios

Teacher: ... Cuando yo era niño, vivíamos cerca de la ciudad donde mi padre tenía negocios.

Class: ... Cuando yo era niño, vivíamos cerca de la ciudad donde mi padre tenía negocios.

B. The above should be used for individual repetition.

C. Teacher, while drilling sentence, shows picture which describes setting. In order to insure that all students have understood the meaning of the sentence, teacher asks: ¿Quién sabe lo que significa la frase en inglés? Who understands the meaning of the sentence? After students have offered explanations, the teacher gives the English meaning.

D. Teacher writes the sentence on the board, underlining the three examples of the imperfect tense. The teacher explains that ⟨era⟩ is the first person singular imperfect tense of ⟨ser⟩ which will be treated later. The class will presently deal with ⟨vivir⟩ and ⟨tener⟩, model verbs for the /er/ and /ir/ verb conjugations.

Before the verb structure is explained the teacher uses the model sentence to explain the use of the tense. The verbs in the model sentence are written in the imperfect tense. This tense describes a state or an action which was habitual, repeated or took place

---

[1] The above is a modification of several sentences found in Thompson, Mary P. et al. *Audio-Lingual Materials, Spanish Level Two* (New York, N.Y., 1961), p. 59.

over an indefinite period of time in the past. This idea corresponds to the English "used to", "was + ing form of the verb".

E. 1. Repetition drill of /er/, /ir/ model verb

Teacher	Class
Yo tenía el libro.	Yo tenía el libro.
Tú tenías el libro.	Tú tenías el libro.
Él tenía el libro.	Él tenía el libro.
Ella tenía el libro.	Ella tenía el libro.
Usted tenía el libro.	Usted tenía el libro.
Nosotros teníamos el libro.	Nosotros teníamos el libro.
Vosotros teníais el libro.	Vosotros teníais el libro.
Ellos tenían el libro.	Ellos tenían el libro.
Ellas tenían el libro.	Ellas tenían el libro.
Ustedes tenían el libro.	Ustedes tenían el libro.

2. Substitution drill

Teacher	Class
*Yo ten*ía el libro.	Yo tenía el libro.
Tú_____	Tú tenías el libro.
Él_____	Él tenía el libro.
Ella _____	Ella tenía el libro.
Usted _____	Usted tenía el libro.
Nosotros _____	Nosotros teníamos el libro.
Vosotros _____	Vosotros teníais el libro.
Ellos _____	Ellos tenían el libro.
Ellas _____	Ellas tenían el libro.
Ustedes _____	Ustedes tenían el libro.

3. The teacher writes forms on the blackboard indicating signals related to each subject pronoun. Across from forms for verb ⟨tener⟩, the verb ⟨vivir⟩ should also be written. The teacher should indicate that both /er/ and /ir/ verbs are conjugated in the same manner.

tener	vivir
Yo ten|ía| el libro	Yo viv|ía cerca de la ciudad.
tú ten|ía|s	tú viv|ía|s
él ten|ía	él viv|ía

tener	*vivir*
ella ten|ía	ella viv|ía
usted ten|ía	usted viv|ía
nosotros ten|ía|mos	nosotros viv|ía|mos
vosotros ten|ía|is	vosotros viv|ía|is
ellos ten|ía|n	ellos viv|ía|ns
ellas ten|ía|n	ellas viv|ía|n
ustedes ten|ía|n	ustedes viv|ía|n

MICRO-LESSON 12. (1 1/2)

Goal: Teaching of the imperfect tense: complementary practice of /er/ and /ir/ verbs.

Linguistic Basis: Refer to pp. 19, 20, 30-33

Performance Criteria:

Used in planning: III

Additional references: I, II, VIII

OUTLINE OF LESSON:

A. 1. The teacher presents this short story, reading it twice to the students. As the teacher reads it, he can point to poster cards depicting the story. (Suggestion: poster cards can be made by pasting relevant magazine or newspaper pictures on large pieces of oak tag.)

Cuando *vivo* en Madrid, sigo el siguiente horario. *Suelo* levantarme a las siete y comer un bollo con café a las siete y media. A las ocho, *salgo* para el trabajo. Siendo que *duermo* a pierna suelta, nunca *oigo* el despertador y *tengo* que correr para alcanzar el autobús.

2. The teacher asks for choral repetition and one or two individual repetitions of each of the sentences of the monologue.

B. The teacher insures that students are aware of the action of the story by asking someone to summarize it in English. ¿Hay alguien que nos pueda relatar el cuento en inglés? The teacher explains that "dormir a pierna suelta" is an idiom meaning "to sleep like a log."

C. The teacher contrasts each sentence in the present with the imperfect. The teacher asks for several repetitions of each sentence in the imperfect.

D. The teacher then reads each sentence in the present tense. The teacher asks the class for a choral response in the imperfect: Repitan cada frase usando el tiempo imperfecto. After each response, the teacher writes the present and the corresponding imperfect form.

Cuando vivo en Madrid	Cuando vivía en Madrid
sigo el siguiente horario	seguía el siguiente horario
suelo levantarme	solía levantarme
salgo para el trabajo	salía para el trabajo
duermo a pierna suelta	dormía a pierna suelta
oigo el despertador	oía el despertador
tengo que correr	tenía que correr

E. The teacher then points out the use of the imperfect tense as had been done in the previous lesson. This tense describes a state or an action which was habitual, repeated or took place over an indefinite period of time in the past. This idea corresponds to the English "used to," "was + ing form of the verb."

F. The teacher gives sentences in the present tense and calls on individuals to repeat the sentence, using the imperfect tense of the verb. Choral response can then follow using the same sentences.

Examples:

Teacher cues:	*Response:*
Yo suelo ir al cine.	Yo solía ir al cine.
Él viene a las tres.	Él venía a las tres.
Nosotros comemos en la escuela.	Nosotros comíamos en la escuela.

MICRO-LESSON 13. (1)

Goal: Teaching of the preterite tense: the initial presentation of /ar/ verbs.

Linguistic Basis: Refer to pp. 19, 20, 30-33

Performance Criteria:

Used in planning: III

Additional references: I, II

OUTLINE OF LESSON:

A. Teacher models: Comí la manzana, hablé con mi madre por teléfono y le escribí a mi hermana.
Teacher signals repetition using backward buildup:
...y le escribí a mi hermana
Class: ...y le escribí a mi hermana
Teacher: ...hablé con mi madre por teléfono y le escribí a mi hermana
Class: ...repeats
Teacher: Comí la manzana, hablé con mi madre por teléfono y le escribí a mi hermana.
Class: repeats
B. The above should be used for individual repetition.
C. Teacher acts out the sentence. In order to insure that all students have comprehended the meaning, teacher asks: ¿Quién sabe lo que significa esta frase en inglés? Who knows what this sentence means? After students have volunteered answers, teacher should explain the English meaning.
D. The teacher writes the sentence on the blackboard underlining the verbs. The teacher explains that these verbs are written in the preterite tense, a tense used to show a completed action in the past at a definite point in time.
The verb ⟨hablar⟩ in the sentence will be used as a model for the /ar/ verbs.
E. 1. Repetition drill of /ar/ model verb

Teacher:	*Class:*
Yo hablé con Juan.	Yo hablé con Juan.
tú hablaste con Juan	tú hablaste con Juan
él habló con Juan	él habló con Juan
ella habló con Juan	ella habló con Juan
usted habló con Juan	usted habló con Juan
Nosotros hablamos con Juan.	Nosotros hablamos con Juan.
vosotros hablasteis con Juan	vosotros hablasteis con Juan
ellos hablaron con Juan	ellos hablaron con Juan

ellas hablaron con Juan
ustedes hablaron con
   Juan

ellas hablaron con Juan
ustedes hablaron con
   Juan

2. Substitution drill

Teacher:	*Class:*
Yo hablé con Juan.	Yo hablé con Juan.
tú _____	tú hablaste con Juan
él _____	él habló con Juan
ella _____	ella habló con Juan
usted _____	usted habló con Juan
nosotros _____	nosotros hablamos con Juan
vosotros _____	vosotros hablasteis con Juan
ellos _____	ellos hablaron con Juan
ellas _____	ellas hablaron con Juan
ustedes _____	ustedes hablaron con Juan

3. The teacher writes the forms on the blackboard, indicating signals related to each subject pronoun.

Yo habl|é con Juan	Nosotros habl|a|mos con Juan.
tú habl|aste	vosotros habl|a|steis
él habl|ó	ellos habl|a|ron
ella habl|ó	ellas habl|a|ron
usted habl|ó	ustedes habl|a|ron

MICRO-LESSON 14. (1)

Goal: Teaching of the preterite tense: complementary practice of /ar/ verbs.

Linguistic Basis: Refer to pp. 19, 20, 31-33

Performance Criteria:

    Used in planning: III

    Additional references: I, II, VIII

OUTLINE OF LESSON:

A. 1. The teacher presents this short story, reading it twice to the students. As the teacher reads it, he

/

can point to poster cards depicting the story. (Suggestion: poster cards can be made by pasting magazine or newspaper pictures on large pieces of oak tag.)

Todos los lunes, camino al mercado y compro legumbres, frutas y quesos. Pero antes de pagarle al vendedor discuto el precio, es decir, regateo. Después de la compra, regreso a casa, arreglo un almuerzo bien delicioso y espero a mi marido. En la tarde, empiezo a hacer el ganchillo y bordo el mantel.

2. The teacher asks for choral repetition and one or two individual repetitions of each of the sentences of the monologue.

B. The teacher insures that students are aware of the action of the story by asking someone to summarize it in English. ¿Hay alguien que nos pueda relatar el cuento en inglés? The teacher also explains that the verb *discuitir* does *not* mean *to discuss* but rather to *argue* and that the verb *regatear* means to argue about a price, i.e., to haggle.

C. The teacher contrasts each sentence in the present with the preterite. The teacher asks for several repetitions of each sentence in the preterite. The teacher begins the story with the word *ayer*.

D. The teacher then reads each sentence in the present tense and asks the class for a choral response in the preterite: Repitan cada frase usando el tiempo pretérito. After each response, the teacher writes the present and the corresponding preterite form:

camino al mercado	caminé al mercado
compro legumbres	compré legumbres
regateo	regateé
regreso a casa	regresé a casa
arreglo un almuerzo	arreglé un almuerzo
espero a mi marido	esperé a mi marido
empiezo mis bordados	empecé mis bordados
bordo el mantel	bordé el mantel

E. The teacher then points out the use of the preterite tense as had been done in the previous lesson. The preterite tense is a tense used to show a complete action in the past at a definite point in time.
F. The teacher gives sentences in the present tense and calls on individuals to repeat the sentence using the preterite tense of the verb. Choral response can then follow using the same sentences.
Examples:

Teacher cues	*Response*
Él camina al teatro.	Él caminó al teatro.
Los soldados marchan.	Los soldados marcharon.
Yo compro muchos zapatos.	Yo compré muchos zapatos.

MICRO-LESSON 15. (1)

Goal: Teaching Class 1, /e/ to /ie/ change of radical changing verbs: initial presentation
Linguistic Basis: Refer to p. 24
Performance Criteria:
 Used in planning: III, VIII
 Additional references: I, II

OUTLINE OF LESSON:

A. 1. Teacher points to a boy in the class, then a girl and says:
 Él quiere ir al cine pero ella empieza a cocinar. bi Teacher can use large poster cards illustrating 1 movie and 2) a girl cooking.
 2. Teacher uses backward buildup (two parts are sufficient).
 Teacher cues: ... pero ella empieza a cocinar
 Class: ... repeats
 Teacher cues: Él quiere ir al cine pero ella empiez a cocinar.
 Class: repeats
 3. Teacher models sentence and points to individual students to repeat.

B. The teacher asks: ¿Quién comprende el significado de la frase? Who understands the meaning of the sentence? Teacher can use poster cards to illustrate and finally, give English meaning. (Suggestion: poster cards can be made by pasting relevant magazine or newspaper pictures on large pieces of oak tag.)

C. Teacher

models:	él quiere ir al cine	(signals choral repetition)
Class:	repeats	
Teacher:	tú quieres ir al cine	(teacher points to one student; signals repetition)
Class:	repeats	
Teacher:	Yo quiero ir al cine.	(teacher points to himself; signals repetition)
Class:	repeats	
Teacher:	Nosotros queremos ir al cine.	(teacher points to everyone; signals repetition)
Class:	repeats	
Teacher:	Vosotros queréis ir al cine.	(teacher points to class; signals repetition)
Class:	repeats	
Teacher:	Ellos quieren ir al cine.	(teacher points to a group of students; signals repetition)
Class:	repeats	

D. The teacher models the verb ⟨querer⟩ as in choral repetition and uses same procedure for individual repetition drill.

E. The teacher writes verb ⟨querer⟩ on the board:

Example:		
	Yo quiero	Nosotros queremos
	tú quieres	vosotros queréis
	él quiere	ellos quieren
	ella quiere	ellas quieren
	usted quiere	ustedes quieren

The teacher then asks students to look for a difference among forms. ¿Qué diferencia notan ustedes? Once the students have given the answer in part or in whole, the teacher outlines the radical changing verb forms.

Example:

Yo quiero	Nosotros queremos
tú quieres	vosotros queréis

él quiere	ellos quieren
ella quiere	ellas quieren
usted quiere	ustedes quieren

The teacher explains that the stressed vowel /e/ of the stem ⟨quer⟩ changes to /ie/ due to the stress.

F. The same procedure used for choral and individual repetition with the verb ⟨querer⟩ is now used with the verb ⟨empezar⟩.

Example:

Teacher models:

Ella empieza a cocinar.	(teacher signals repetition and points to a girl)
Class:	repeats
Teacher: Yo empiezo a cocinar	(teacher points to herself and signals repetition)
Class:	repeats

G. The teacher then writes the verb ⟨empezar⟩ on the blackboard:

Example:

Yo empiezo	nosotros empezamos
tú empiezas	vosotros empezáis
él empieza	ellos empiezan
ella empieza	ellas empiezan
usted empieza	ustedes empiezan

The teacher asks students to look for a difference among forms ¿Qué diferencia notan ustedes? Once the students have given the answer in part or in whole, the teacher outlines radical changing verb forms.

Yo empiezo	nosotros empezamos
tú empiezas	vosotros empezáis

él empieza	ellos empiezan
ella empieza	ellas empiezan
usted empieza	ustedes empiezan

The teacher explains that the stress vowel /e/ of the stem ⟨empez⟩ changes to /ie/ because of the stress. The teacher explains that the verbs ⟨querer⟩ and ⟨empezar⟩ are examples of /er/ and /ar/ verbs in Class 1 radical changing verbs in which the stem vowel /e/ changes when stressed to /ie/.

H. Teacher uses number substitution drill to review verbs. Teacher instructs students that if the cue is the singular verb form, the students are to change it to its corresponding plural form, i.e., if the cue is in the first person plural form, the students are to change it to the first person singular form and vice versa. Teacher helps the students during the first part of the drill in order to establish the pattern.

Teacher:	*Students:*
Empezamos a cocinar.	Empiezo a cocinar.
Empezáis a cocinar.	Empiezas a cocinar.
Empieza a cocinar.	Empiezan a cocinar. etc.
Quiero ir al cine.	Queremos ir al cine.
Queremos ir al cine.	Quiero ir al cine.
Quieren ir al cine.	Quiere ir al cine. etc.

Micro-lesson 15a. (1) Homework

Goal: Related homework assignment.
Linguistic Basis: Refer to p. 24
Performance Criteria:
    Used in planning: X
    Additional references: I, II, III

Assignment:

In order to reinforce the material presented in class, the teacher distributes a work sheet of verb forms. The students are to fill in the forms for the verbs which include ⟨querer⟩, ⟨empezar⟩ and other /ar/ and /er/ radical changing verbs of the same class. The forms, one for each verb, are modeled according to the following example:

Pensar

stem _____	radical vowel_____
yo	nosotros
tú	vosotros
él	ellos
ella	ellas
usted	ustedes

The verb form is then to be written as follows:

nosotros	vosotros
ellos	ella
usted	ustedes
tú	él
yo	ellas

Utility of the assignment:

Once all the radical changing verbs have been taught, a comparable assignment can be made based on this model including all previously taught radical changing verbs.

MICRO-LESSON 16. (1)

Goal: Teaching Class 1, /e/ to /ie/ change of radical changing verbs: complementary practice.

Linguistic Basis: Refer to p. 24

Performance Criteria:
    Used in planning: III
    Additional references: I, II, X

OUTLINE OF LESSON:

A. Substitution drill

Teacher cues:	*Class:*
Empezar:	
yo empiezo a cocinar	yo empiezo a cocinar
nosotros _____	nosotros empezamos a cocinar
ellos _____	ellos empiezan a cocinar
ellas _____	ellas empiezan a cocinar

Teacher cues:	*Class:*
ustedes _____	ustedes empiezan a cocinar
vosotros _____	vosotros empezáis a cocinar
tú _____	tú empiezas a cocinar
él _____	él empieza a cocinar
ella _____	ella empieza a cocinar
usted _____	usted empieza a cocinar

Querer:

nosotros queremos ir al cine	nosotros queremos ir al cine
tú _____	tú quieres ir al cine
vosotros _____	vosotros queréis ir al cine
ellos _____	ellos quieren ir al cine
ellas _____	ellas quieren ir al cine
ustedes _____	ustedes quieren ir al cine
yo _____	yo quiero ir al cine
él _____	él quiere ir al cine

B. Number substitution

Teacher uses other verbs of the same class of radical changing verbs. The teacher instructs students that if the cue is the singular verb form, the students are to change it to its corresponding plural form, i.e., if the cue is in the first person plural form, the students are to change it to the first person singular form and vice versa. The teacher helps the students during the first part of the drill in order to establish the pattern.

Pensar:

Pensamos bien de ella.	Pienso bien de ella.
Pensáis bien de ella.	Piensas bien de ella.
Piensa bien de ella.	Piensan bien de ella.

Sentar:

Se sienta en la silla cómoda.	Se sientan en la silla cómoda.
Os sentáis en la silla cómoda.	Te sientas en la silla cómoda.
Nos sentamos en la silla cómoda.	Me siento en la silla cómoda.

Entender:

No entendéis lo que dice.	No entiendes lo que dice.
No entendemos lo que dice.	No entiendo lo que dice.
No entienden lo que dice.	No entiende lo que dice.

C. Transformation drill

The teacher tells the students that they are to transform the infinitive verb forms to correspond to the person of the conjugated verb in each of the model sentences.

Example: model sentence: quiero *extender* la cuerda.
Extender is the infinitive which changes to: *extiendo* la cuerda.

EMPEZAR

Teacher cues:	*Class:*
podemos empezar a leer	empezamos a leer
pueden empezar a leer	empiezan a leer
puedes empezar a leer	empiezas a leer
puedo empezar a leer	empiezo a leer
podéis empezar a leer	empezáis a leer
puede empezar a leer	empieza a leer

SENTAR

Teacher cues:	*Class:*
podemos sentarnos allí	nos sentamos allí
podéis sentaros allí	os sentáis allí
puede sentarse allí	se sienta allí
puedes sentarte allí	te sientas allí
puedo sentarme allí	me siento allí
pueden sentarse allí	se sientan allí

D. Teacher distributes dittoed sheet of transformation and substitution exercises of material drilled orally. Exercise sheet should only include column of cues and opposite each cue a blank to be filled in by the student.

Example:

Number substitution:

pensamos bien de ella	_____
pensáis bien de ella	_____
piensa bien de ella	_____

MICRO-LESSON 17. (1) TEST

Goal: Test on Class 1, /e/ to /ie/ change of radical changing
verbs.
Linguistic Basis: Refer to p. 24
Performance Criteria:
Used in planning: XI
Additional references: I, II, III

TEST

The teacher administers an examination to test the comprehension of the previously taught radical changing verbs
(/e/−/ie/ change in Class 1). The test is based on the substitution and transformation drills used in classwork.
Sample items can be constructed as follows:

1. *Number substitution*

Directions: Students are to substitute the corresponding
singular form for the given plural and the corresponding
plural form for any given singular.
Example: *Nosotros hablamos* is changed to *Yo hablo*.
Sample item:

Entender−nosotros entendemos   _____
vosotros entendéis   _____
él entiende   _____

The above form may be used with other verbs of the
same verb class for this particular test.

2. *Transformation*

Directions: Students are to transform infinitive verb
forms to correspond to the person of the conjugated verb
in each of the model sentences.
Example: model sentence: Quiero *extender* la cuerda.
Extender is the infinitive which changes to:
extiendo la cuerda.
Sample item:

Negar−no podéis negar la verdad   _____
no puedo negar la verdad   _____
no pueden negar la verdad   _____

3. *Transformation*

Answer the following questions incorporating the verb in the question.
Sample items:
1) ¿Entiendes lo que ha dicho el señor?
2) ¿Ella empieza la cena a las siete?
3) ¿Niegan haberlo dicho?
4) ¿Qué piensas de la película?
5) ¿Qué quieres?

4. *Utility of the test*

Once all radical changing verbs have been taught, the teacher administers a test based on this model, including all radical changing verbs previously taught.

MICRO-LESSON 18. (1 1/2)

Goal: Teaching the imperfect—preterite contrast
Linguistic Basis: Refer to pp. 26, 31-33
Performance Criteria:
    Used in planning: III
    Additional references: I

OUTLINE OF LESSON:

A. Teacher models the following sentences for the students, asking for choral repetition and individual repetition after each one.
    Mientras que la maestra no miraba, el niño tiró el libro.
    Un día, cuando Ramón caminaba a la escuela, se le cayeron las gafas.
    Cuando ella se lo preguntó, él no sabía que decir.
B. Teacher makes certain that all students understand the meaning of the sentence by asking them to explain the idea expressed in the sentences. ¿Quién nos puede explicar la idea expresada en cada frase?
C. Teacher models each sentence explaining the use of the imperfect, the use of the preterite and their interrelationship. The teacher follows the outlined procedure:

1) Teacher models: Mientras que la maestra no miraba
...Teacher explains that ⟨*miraba*⟩ is an action which took place over an indefinite period of time in the past.

Teacher models: ... el niño tiró el libro. Then, explains that ⟨*tiró*⟩ is a completed action at a definite point in time in the past which happened while the teacher wasn't looking.

If it were to be drawn, it would look like this:

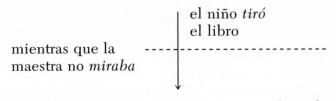

2) Teacher models: ... cuando Ramón caminaba a la escuela... Teacher explains that ⟨*caminaba*⟩ is an action which took place over an indefinite period of time in the past.

Teacher reads: ... se le cayeron las gafas ... and explains that ⟨*cayeron*⟩ is a completed action at a definite point in time in the past. It happened *while* the boy was walking to school.

If it were to be drawn, it would look like this:

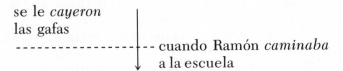

3) Teacher models: ... cuando ella se lo preguntó ... explaining that ⟨*preguntó*⟩ is a completed action at a definite point in time in the past. She asked the question and the action of asking was completely finished.

Teacher models: ... él no sabía que decir ... explaining that ⟨*sabía*⟩ describes the state of not knowing, which took place over an indefinite period of time in the past.

If it were to be drawn, it would look like this:
preguntó

no *sabía* que decir

- -

D. Expansion

Teacher instructs students that they are to complete the phrases orally. After having done so, they are to explain the relationship of one action to another. The teacher calls on individual students.

Example:

Teacher cues: Mientras que ella lavaba la ropa...

Student: Mientras que ella lavaba la ropa, su hermano entró en la casa.

Student should then explain: ⟨*lavaba*⟩ is an action which took place over an indefinite period of time and ⟨*entró*⟩ is the completed action which took place while the clothes were being washed.

Sample items:

1) Alberto estaba durmiendo...
2) Cuando ella llegó de compras...
3) El niñito dormía en su cuna...
4) Ella compró dos vestidos...
5) Mientras que ellos estudiaban...

MICRO-LESSON 19. (1 1/2)

Goal: Use of subjunctive in noun clauses; restricted to examples using verbs of doubt and emotion in independent clauses. It is assumed that students are already familiar with subjunctive forms.

Linguistic Basis: Refer to p. 35

Performance Criteria:

Used in planning: III

Additional references: I, II

OUTLINE OF LESSON:

A. Teacher models pairs of sentences:

Sé que vienes.   Ojalá que vengas.

Sé que vienes.	Espero que vengas.
No dudo que viene.	Dudo que venga.
Creo que vienen.	No creo que vengan.
Es seguro que vienes.	Es posible que vengas.

B. Teacher asks for choral and individual repetitions of each pair of sentences as she models them.

C. Teacher writes 3 or 4 pairs on the board:

Sé que vienes.	Ojalá que vengas.
Sé que vienes.	Espero que vengas.
No dudo que vienes.	Dudo que venga.
Es seguro que venimos.	Es posible que vengamos.

Teacher asks students to identify the basic observable differences in each pair of sentences. En cada par de frases hay ciertas diferencias esenciales, ¿cuales son? Teacher then explains that the subjunctive is required after verbs of doubt and emotion.

D. Transformation Drill:

Teacher gives cue sentence using the indicative in noun clause. Teacher calls on individual students to give parallel constructions using the subjunctive.

Example:

Teacher cues: Sé que vienes.

Student: Espero que vengas. or Es posible que vengas.

Sample items:

Teacher cues:	*Student response:*
Sé que vienes.	Espero que vengas.
Es seguro que vendremos.	Es posible que vengamos.
No hay duda que viene.	Dudo que venga.
Creo que vienen.	No creo que vengan.

MICRO-LESSON 20. (1 1/2)

Goal: Test on the use of the subjunctive in noun clauses; restricted to examples using verbs of doubt and emotion in independent clauses.

Linguistic Basis: Refer to p. 35

Performance Criteria:

Used in planning: XI

TEST

The teacher administers an examination testing the students' grasp of the previously taught concept; use of the subjunctive in noun clauses using verbs of doubt and emotion in independent clauses. The test includes exercises used in class and other exercises which measure comprehension of the above concept.

1. Transformation:

   Directions: Students are to transform the indicative phrase to a comparable phrase requiring the use of the subjunctive.

   Sample items:

Indicative	*Subjunctive*
No dudo que come mucho.	_____
Sé que duerme mucho.	_____
Creo que vienen hoy.	_____
Es seguro que habla mucho.	_____

2. Substitution:

   Directions: Students are to supply the correct verb form.

   Sample items:

   Es posible que tú _____. (fracasar)

   Dudo que él _____. (estudiar)

   Sé que nosotros _____aquí. (vivir)

MICRO-LESSON 21. (1)

Goal: Teaching the subject-object reversal: gustar, parecer, encantar, faltar.

Linguistic Basis: Refer to pp. 43, 44

Performance Criteria:

   Used in planning: III

   Additional references: I, II

OUTLINE OF LESSON:

A. Teacher models basic sentences signalling choral and individual repetition:

   Me encanta ese vestido de seda.

   Te faltan diez dólares para comprarlo.

La muchacha les parece bonita.

A José Manuel le gusta la morena.

B. Person-number substitution (choral followed by individual participation).

Teacher cues:	*Student response:*
GUSTAR	
A mí me gusta la morena.	A mí me gusta la morena.
A ti _____.	A ti te gusta la morena.
A él _____.	A él le gusta la morena.
A nosotros _____.	A nosotros nos gusta la morena.
A vosotros _____.	A vosotros os gusta la morena.
A ellos _____.	A ellos les gusta la morena.
A José Manuel _____.	A José Manuel le gusta la morena.
ENCANTAR	
A mí me encanta ese vestido de seda.	A mí me encanta ese vestido de seda.
A ti _____.	A ti te encanta ese vestido de seda.
A él _____.	A él le encanta ese vestido de seda.
A nosotros _____.	A nosotros nos encanta ese vestido de seda.
A vosotros _____.	A vosotros os encanta ese vestido de seda.
A ellos _____.	A ellos les encanta ese vestido de seda.
FALTAR	
A mí me faltan diez dólares.	A mí me faltan diez dólares.
A ti _____.	A ti te faltan diez dólares.
A él _____.	A él le faltan diez dólares.
A nosotros _____.	A nosotros nos faltan diez dólares.
A vosotros _____.	A vosotros os faltan diez dólares.

Teacher cues:	*Student response:*
A ellos _____.	A ellos les faltan diez dólares.

PARECER

A mí la muchacha me parece bonita.	A mí la muchacha me parece bonita.
A ti _____.	A ti la muchacha te parece bonita.
a él _____.	A él la muchacha le parece bonita.
A nosotros _____.	A nosotros la muchacha nos parece bonita.
A vosotros _____.	A vosotros la muchacha os parece bonita.
A ellos _____.	A ellos la muchacha les parece bonita.

C. Response Drill: Teacher points to individual students asking them a question based on the above drills. Teacher helps students in initial stages of drill.

Sample items:

Teacher asks:	*Possible student response:*
¿Por qué no compras el vestido?	Por que me faltan diez dólares.
¿Por qué te pones el vestido?	Por que me gusta.
¿Por qué vas al cine esta noche?	Por que me encanta la película.
¿Por qué sale José Manuel con esa chica?	Por que le parece encantadora.

MICRO-LESSON 22. (1/2)

Goal: Point out lack of Spanish-English pattern correspondence in expressions of weather.
Linguistic Basis: Refer to pp. 50, 51
Performance Criteria:
   Used in planning: III
   Additional references: I, II, VIII

OUTLINE OF LESSON:

A. Teacher reads sentences to students. Drawings or pictures depicting sunny weather, rainy weather, etc. can be used to convey meaning.

Hace sol.	Hace buen día.	Está nevando.
Hace frío.	Hace mal tiempo.	Está lloviendo.
Hace calor.	Hace mal día.	(llueve)
Hace buen tiempo.		Hay neblina.

B. Teacher asks for choral repetition. For individual participation, the teacher asks each student ¿Qué tiempo hace hoy? To cue the students, the teacher points to one of the pictures used previously (i.e., a picture of good weather should elicit: ⟨Hace buen tiempo⟩, or ⟨Hace sol⟩, or ⟨Hace buen día⟩).

C. Teacher writes several expressions on the board: two or three using ⟨hace⟩ and two or three which do not use ⟨hace⟩.

Hace buen día.	Llueve.
Hace mal tiempo.	Está nevando.
Hace calor.	Hay neblina.

Teacher explains that in English, the expressions of weather are uniformly denoted by "It is" whereas in Spanish, expressions of weather lack uniformity.

D. As a review, teacher asks each student ¿Qué tiempo hace hoy? pointing to the pictures or out the window as a cue.

E. Teacher asks students questions which the student can answer according to a real situation. (situational cue)

Sample items:

Teacher asks:	*Student response:*
¿Cuándo vas a la playa?	Cuando hace buen tiempo.
¿Por qué sales?	Porque hace sol.
¿No vas a la tienda?	¡No! Está lloviendo.
¿Quieres ir al centro?	¡No! Porque hace mal tiempo.

MICRO-LESSON 23. (1/2)

Goal: Teaching personal ⟨a⟩ (assuming contraction a + el = al has been taught).

Linguistic Basis: Refer to p. 52

Performance Criteria:

Used in planning: III

Additional references: I, II

OUTLINE OF LESSON:

A. Teacher models sentences:

Él busca la novela.	Él busca a María.
Él prefiere las papas fritas.	Él prefiere a las morenas.
Él ve los libros.	Él ve a los profesores.

B. Students repeat sentence in choral repetition and in individual repetition.

C. Teacher models each pair of sentences and after each pair asks students what difference they perceive. After a one minute discussion, the teacher points out that when the object is a person, it is preceded by ⟨a⟩. The verbs ⟨tener⟩ and ⟨haber⟩ are exceptions.

Examples: Yo tengo tres hijos.

Hay dos muchachas en la tienda.

D. Teacher writes one or two of the above sentences on the board (or uses an overhead projector if sentences are already written out). Teacher then points out differences.

E. Substitution Drill:

Directions: Teacher gives model sentence and then gives cue only. Students are to complete structure according to the original pattern using ⟨a⟩ whenever necessary.

Teacher cues:	*Student response:*
Yo busco al profesor.	Yo busco al profesor.
_____ hombre.	Yo busco al hombre.
_____ libro.	Yo busco el libro.
_____ señora.	Yo busco a la señora.
_____ escuela.	Yo busco la escuela.
_____ niña.	Yo busco a la niña.

Teacher cues:	*Student response:*
_____ teléfono.	Yo busco el teléfono.
_____ El Prado.	Yo busco El Prado.
_____ médico.	Yo busco al médico.

F. Response Drill:

Teacher asks each student a question. Student should use personal ⟨a⟩ whenever necessary. A variety of answers is acceptable.

Sample items:

Teacher cues:	*Possible student response:*
¿Qué buscas en la escuela?	Busco el libro.
¿Qué prefieres comer?	Prefiero helado.
¿A quién prefieres, a la rubia o a la morena?	Prefiero a la rubia.
¿Por qué estás en la biblioteca ahora?	Porque espero a María.
¿Por qué está Juan allí?	Porque quiere ver al cartero.

MICRO-LESSON 24. (1 1/2)

Goal: Teaching the reflexive construction for use in impersonal expressions.

Linguistic Basis: Refer to pp. 47, 48

Performance Criteria:

Used in planning: III

Additional references: I, II

OUTLINE OF LESSON:

A. Teacher models the following pairs of sentences:

Ella come bien en ese restaurante.

Se come bien en ese restaurante.

Nosotros dormimos bien en ese hotel.

Se duerme bien en ese hotel.

Ellos trabajan mucho en la Universidad.

Se trabaja mucho en la Universidad.

B. Teacher models sentences for students to repeat, first chorally and then individually.

C. Teacher writes sentences on the board. Teacher explains to students that verbs which are not reflexive (e.g., ⟨comer, dormir⟩ as opposed to ⟨lavarse, vestirse⟩) can be conjugated in the third person singular or plural according to the reflexive pattern in order to express an impersonal situation.

Teacher uses examples on board to clarify:

Example: Se vende papel.

Vender is not a reflexive verb but has been conjugated in the third person singular according to the reflexive pattern in order to express an impersonal situation. Using the same example, the teacher explains that the verb is conjugated in the third person singular and/or plural: e.g. ⟨se vende papel; se venden huevos⟩.

D. Transformation Exercise:

Teacher cues students by using sentences in the present tense. Students transform sentences to the impersonal reflexive.

Teacher cues:	*Student response:*
Los aldeanos venden huevos en el mercado.	Se venden huevos en el mercado.
Yo consigo papel allí.	Se consigue papel allí.
Ellos compran cigarros.	Se compran cigarros.
Nosotros hablamos inglés en la escuela.	Se habla inglés en la escuela.

E. Translation Drill:

Students are to translate English sentences to Spanish according to model Spanish sentence.

Teacher cues:	*Student response:*
Vegetables sold here.	Se venden legumbres.
Meat sold here.	Se vende carne.
Tacos sold here.	Se venden tacos.
Can one enter?	¿Se puede entrar?
Can one swim here?	¿Se puede nadar aquí?

MICRO-LESSON 25. (1)

Goal: Teaching ⟨conocer/saber⟩ distinction: different lexical items correspond to a given English item.

Linguistic Basis: Refer to pp. 53-55

Performance Criteria:
    Used in planning: III
    Additional references: I, II

OUTLINE OF LESSON:

A. Teacher models sentences using ⟨conocer⟩ and ⟨saber⟩:
    María conoce al professor.
    María sabe que el profesor está en casa.
    Juan conoce al señor García.
    Juan sabe que el señor García vive en Madrid.
    Nosotros conocemos la ciudad de Madrid.
    Nosotros sabemos que Madrid está en España.
B. Students repeat sentences in choral and individual repetition.
C. Teacher writes sentences on the board and gives English meaning orally for each sentence. Teacher points out that although ⟨conocer⟩ and ⟨saber⟩ both mean "to know", ⟨conocer⟩ is used with a direct object and generally indicates knowing a person, place or thing. ⟨Saber⟩ is followed by ⟨que⟩ and a *subordinate clause* (saber + que = subordinate clause) and generally indicates knowing a fact. ⟨Saber⟩ can also be followed by an infinitive to indicate a particular skill. (e.g. Sé hablar inglés.)
D. Substitution Drill:
    Directions: Students are to use the verbs ⟨saber⟩ or ⟨conocer⟩ and complete the sentence accordingly. The first person singular of the verb form will be used.

    Sample items:

Teacher cues:	*Student response:*
Conozco al profesor.	Conozco al profesor.
_____ que viene.	Sé que viene.
_____ que se marcha.	Sé que se marcha.
_____ la ciudad de Barcelona.	Conozco la ciudad de Barcelona.
_____ a la familia Conde.	Conozco a la familia Conde.

E. Teacher models the following sentences using ⟨conocer⟩ and ⟨saber⟩.

Conozco la historia de España.	Sé la historia de España.
Conozco el cuento.	Sé el cuento.
Conozco la música de los mariachis.	Sé la música de los mariachis.

F. Students repeat sentences in choral and individual repetition.

G. Teacher writes sentences on the board. Teacher explains that ⟨conocer⟩ and ⟨saber⟩ can be used with a direct object. The essential difference is a semantic one and an important one.

⟨conocer⟩ + direct object = to have an acquaintance with something; to have a general idea of what is being spoken about

⟨saber⟩ + direct object = to know something thoroughly

Teacher explains that the speaker must make the distinction in his own mind and must remember that if something is structurally sensible, it is not necessarily semantically correct. An example from English:

I will pick up the book.	(structurally and semantically correct)
I will pick up the mountain.	(structurally correct; semantically nonsensical)

H. Response Drills:

Directions: Teacher asks individual students questions in which they are to practice the correct use of ⟨saber⟩ and ⟨conocer⟩. After each utterance, student can explain use of ⟨saber⟩ and ⟨conocer⟩.

Sample items:

1) ¿Conoces el Poema del Cid?
2) ¿Sabes la asignatura?
3) ¿Qué sabes de la historia de España?
4) ¿Conoces la revista esa?
5) ¿Sabrá algo de arquitectura?

MICRO-LESSON 26. (1) TEST

Goal: Testing the correct use of ⟨saber⟩ and ⟨conocer⟩
Linguistic Basis: Refer to pp. 53-55
Performance Criteria:
    Used in planning: XI
Additional references: I, II, III

OUTLINE OF LESSON:

A. Complete the following sentences using ⟨saber⟩ or
    ⟨conocer⟩. (Use the first person singular.)
    Sample items:
        1. _____ que llega.
        2. _____ hablar español.
        3. _____ a esos chicos.
        4. _____ al estudiante.
        5. _____ de donde viene él.
B. Student is to translate and to justify briefly the use of
    the verb ⟨saber⟩ or ⟨conocer⟩.
    1. I know that geography   (Conozco el libro de
        book.   geografía.)
    2. I know history of art.   (Sé la historia del arte.)
    3. I know that gentleman.   (Conozco a ese señor.)
    4. I know that he is coming. (Sé que viene.)
    5. I know how to ski.   (Sé esquiar.)

MICRO-LESSON 27. (1)

Goal: Teaching false cognates.
Linguistic Basis: Refer to p. 59
Performance Criteria:
    Used in planning: VII
    Additional references: II

OUTLINE OF LESSON:

A. Teacher models the following sentences in which the
    cognates are contained:
        No voy a la biblioteca porque he comprado el libro
        en la *librería.*
        En su *conferencia,* el profesor habló de sus *lec-
        turas* de historia.

Voy a ayudar a mi hermano; no puedo *asistir* al
concierto.*

B. Students repeat each sentence chorally and individually.
C. Teacher writes sentences on the board and explains
their meaning. Teacher explains that although many
words in Spanish and English are true cognates
(orthographically and semantically same), there are
some that are not true cognates. These are false cognates and although they are orthographically similar,
semantically there is no relationship (except historical). The words must not be confused with their
English look alikes.

wrong meaning relationship		true meaning relationship	
Spanish cognate	corresponding English meaning	English cognate	corresponding Spanish meaning
alumno	student	alumnus	graduado
conferencia	lecture	conference	conferencia
asistir	attend	assist	ayudar
lecturas	readings	lectures	conferencias
listo (a) (adj.)	ready	list	lista (noun)

D. Response Drills:
Directions: Teacher asks questions individually. Students should try to incorporate the above
cognates into their answers.
Sample Questions:
1) ¿Dónde se compran libros?
2) ¿Dónde se venden libros?

---

* Sentences taken from: Robert L. Politzer and Charles N. Staubach,
Teaching Spanish: A Linguistic Orientation. Revised Edition. (New York,
New York, 1965), p. 163.

3) ¿Qué hacen los profesores en sus clases?
4) ¿A quién enseño yo matemáticas?
5) ¿Qué piensan hacer esta noche?

E. Teacher asks individual students the meaning of the following words. Students are to use these words in a complete sentence.

⟨alumno⟩ ⟨conferencia⟩ ⟨asistir⟩ ⟨lecturas⟩
⟨graduado⟩ ⟨ayudar⟩

Sample Answers:

alumno — student; it is not an alumnus of a school
  1. Un alumno es un estudiante.
conferencia — lecture; can also mean a conference
  2. La conferencia del profesor era muy interesante.
asistir — to attend a play, concert, etc.
  3. Yo asisto a los conciertos del domingo.
lecturas — readings
  4. Yo he hecho las lecturas del curso.
graduado — an alumnus of a university
  5. Yo soy graduada de Rosemont College en Pennsylvania.
ayudar — to help; to assist
  6. Yo ayudo a mi madre con las tareas de la casa.

MICRO-LESSON 28. (1/2)

Goal: Sensitizing students to semantic difference found in the use of the predicate adjective with ⟨ser⟩ and ⟨estar⟩.

Linguistic Basis: Refer to pp. 57-59
Performance Criteria:
  Used in planning: VII
  Additional references: I, II

OUTLINE OF LESSON:
A. Teacher models patterns in which the use of ⟨ser⟩ + adjective is contrasted with ⟨estar⟩ + adjective.
  Eugenia es agradable, pero hoy está más agradable que nunca.
  Manuel y Ramón son simpáticos, pero ahora están más simpáticos.

Isabel y yo somos alegres; ahora estamos más alegres que nunca.

B. Students repeat above patterns first in choral repetition then individually.

C. Teacher writes the patterns on the board. Teacher explains that there is a difference when an adjective is used with ⟨ser⟩ and when it is used with ⟨estar⟩. With ⟨ser⟩ (teacher points to example), it is meant that the adjective becomes part of a person: e.g. Eugenia es agradable. Eugenia siempre es agradable. ⟨Agradable⟩ denotes a permanent and inherent quality of Eugenia.

With ⟨estar⟩, it is meant that the quality denoted by the adjective is only a part of the person for a short while: e.g.... ⟨hoy está más agradable que nunca⟩. Eugenia is usually a pleasant person but today for some reason she is much more so than usual; today's pleasantness is not an integral part of Eugenia's personality.

Teacher summarizes the essential contrast: The inherent attribute of the person himself (⟨ser⟩ + adjective) versus the temporary quality which exists for a fleeting moment (⟨estar⟩ + adjective).

D. Pattern completion:

Teacher calls on individual students and asks each one to complete the model pattern with one of the following adjectives:

Model pattern: Él   él
Ellos ser   adj. pero hoy ellos estar adj. .

⟨feo; guapo; simpático; pesado; inteligente; tonto⟩

MICRO-LESSON 29. (1 1/2)

Goal: Teaching a short reading passage and utilizing it for conversational practice.

Performance Criteria:

Used in planning: VI

OUTLINE OF LESSON:

A. Teacher presents reading passage* to class. Teacher first reads entire selection and then reads each line twice signalling choral repetition.
— ¡Mi general!
— ¡Coronel!
— Es mi deber comunicarle que ocurren cosas muy particulares en el campamento.
— Diga usted, coronel.
— Se sabe, de una manera positiva, que uno de nuestros soldados se sintió al principio un poco enfermo; luego, crecio su enfermedad, más tarde, sintió un terrible dolor en el estómago y por fin vomitó tres cuervos vivos.
— ¿Vomitó qué?
— Tres cuervos, mi general.

B. Teacher then reads the passage, sentence by sentence explaining words which seem unclear. Visual aids, such as posters (e.g. relevant pictures posted on oak tag), free-hand drawings on the blackboard should be used.

C. Teacher instructs students to open their books. Teacher reads each sentence and signals choral and individual repetition. After the selection has been read, individuals are asked to read the passage. Teacher corrects any pronunciation errors, asking individuals to repeat the word or sentence correctly and then asking for choral repetition.

D. Teacher asks questions about passage — the questions, directed at individual students, are of the ⟨yes⟩ and ⟨no⟩ type and are to be answered in complete sentences.

Sample items:

¿El coronel habla con el general?
— Sí, el coronel habla con el general.

---

* Passage taken from: Robert Lado et al. *Galería Hispánica.* (New York, New York, 1965), p. 9.

¿Es el deber del coronel comunicarle al general que
ocurren cosas particulares?
　　　—Sí, es el deber del coronel comunicarle al general
　　　que ocurren cosas particulares.
¿El soldado se sintió bien?
　　　—No, el soldado no se sintió bien.
¿El soldado se sintió enfermo?
　　　—Sí, el soldado se sintió enfermo.
¿Mas tarde, sintió un dolor en el estómago?
　　　—Sí, sintió un dolor en el estómago.
¿Vomitó dos vacas?
　　　—No, no vomitó dos vacas.
¿Vomitó tres gatos?
　　　—No, no vomitó tres gatos.
¿Vomitó tres cuervos?
　　　—Sí, vomitó tres cuervos.

E. Teacher asks questions which involve answering in a
complete sentence.
¿Qué vomitó el soldado?
　　　—El soldado vomitó tres cuervos.
¿Con quién habló el coronel?
　　　—El coronel habló con el general.
¿Cómo se sintió el soldado?
　　　—El soldado se sintió mal.
¿Más tarde, qué es lo que sintió el soldado?
　　　—Más tarde, el soldado sintió un dolor de estó-
　　　mago.

Micro-lesson 30. (1/2)

Goal: Use of tape recorder in introduction of new dia-
logue.
Performance Criteria:
　　　Used in planning: II, IX
Additional references: I, III

Outline of lesson:

A. The teacher will have the tape recorder in such a position that it is in the center of attention. The machine
should be threaded and warmed up before the lesson

begins. The moment the Play button is pressed the dialogue should begin. (Students should not be made to listen to statements about copyright laws in English.) There has been no previous announcement that the students will hear a new dialogue.

Tape: Oye, ¿dónde queda la biblioteca?
      Allí, delante. ¿Vas ahora mismo?
      Sí, tengo que buscar un libro.*

Teacher: (stops the machine): ¿Han comprendido? Did you understand that? (Probable reaction from class will be laughter.) ¿Por qué no? Why not? It's simple: Tomás asks Paco where the library is and Paco tells him. Paco asks him if he's going there right away. Tomás says yes, he has to get a book and so on.
        Teacher tells the class to listen—escuchen. Teacher models the lines and then starts the tape recorder.

B. The tape at this point models and drills the first line of the dialogue. As soon as the model line has been spoken, the teacher stops the machine and takes over the modelling himself. He repeats the line several times and then asks the students to repeat. At this time it is important that the teacher introduce variations of the basic structures underlying the sentences.

Teacher: Oye, ¿dónde queda la biblioteca?
Class: repeats
Teacher: Oye, ¿dónde queda la casa?
Class: repeats
Teacher: Oye, ¿dónde queda el cine?
Class: repeats
Teacher: Oye, ¿dónde queda la biblioteca?
Class: repeats

Teacher will then start the tape recorder again and lead the students in the repetition. As soon as the next line

---

* Dialogue taken from: Mary P. Thompson et al. *Audio-Lingual Materials, Spanish Level One.* (New York, New York, 1961), p. 5.

has been modelled by the taped voice he will stop
the machine and once again take over the teaching
process.

C. The teacher moves the tape back to the point where
the modelling and drill begins and starts playing the
tape. While the tape is playing, the teacher moves
around the room and listens to as many students as
possible, rewarding correct utterances and encouraging the less able students.

D. When the drill session for the first segment of dialogue
is over the tape will repeat the entire segment. The
teacher points out to the class that now that they
know what is being said, they can understand it

MICRO-LESSON 31.

Goal: Teaching a song.
Performance Criteria:
Used in planning: VII

OUTLINE OF LESSON:

A. Teacher tells students that they will learn one verse of
a song, a folksong from the north of Spain. The song
is a story about a pretty young girl (una gachi) who
went to help a young boy who fell from an olive tree.
Later, they fell in love and were married.
Teacher models the first verse and then models one
line at a time:
Students repeat each line chorally:
"Al olivo, al olivo,
al olivo subí;
por cortar una rama
del olivo caí"   (entire text below)

B. Teacher writes words to the first verse on the board.
Teacher models lines pointing to each one while saying it. Students repeat the lines one at a time after
each has been modelled by the teacher.

C. Teacher can sing the first verse, ask students to listen
and then ask them to try to follow along while she

sings. Teacher can motion to student to sing. Gradually, the majority of the students will partake in the singing. (A piano or a guitar would be helpful.)

Text: "Al olivo, al olivo,
al olivo subí;
por cortar una rama
del olivo caí.

Del olivo caí,
quien me levantará;
una gachí morena
que la mano me da.

Que la mano me da,
que la mano me dio;
una gachí morena
es la que quiero yo.

Es la que quiero yo,
es la que he de querer,
esa gachí morena
ha de ser mi mujer."

—NOTES—

—NOTES—

—NOTES—

—NOTES—